MW01503353

HANDBOOK OF THE
MARTIAL ARTS
AND
SELF-DEFENSE

HANDBOOK OF THE
MARTIAL ARTS
AND
SELF-DEFENSE

William Logan and Herman Petras

FUNK & WAGNALLS
New York

ALL PHOTOGRAPHS ARE BY WOODY GOLDBERG AND JOSEPH GRIFFITH.

DESIGNED BY ABIGAIL MOSELEY

Manufactured in the United States of America

Library of Congress Cataloging in Publication Data

Logan, William.
  Handbook of the martial arts and self-defense.

  Bibliography: p.
  Includes index.
  1. Self-defense. I. Petras, Herman, joint author.
II. Title.
GV1111.L63   796.8'15   74-26776
ISBN 0-308-10104-9

1 2 3 4 5 6 7 8 9 10

CONTENTS

INTRODUCTION

The martial arts are not merely self-defense techniques designed to make invincible weapons of the hands and feet. They are a formulated means by which one can attain through diligent practice: a high level of physical proficiency, a tranquil yet superior mental discipline, and a measurable degree of spiritual enlightenment. They are a uniquely structured art form as well as a sport, and seek to develop within the practitioner the principles of sound moral character.

Because they were practiced in strictest secrecy, with little said and even less written about them in their infancy, there's virtually nothing in the way of evidence to prove just when the various styles of the martial arts as we know them today got their start. However, in the sifting of myth from what is mathematically probable, some facts concerning the origins of the martial arts can be determined.

As far back as 5000 B.C. there allegedly existed in India a system of weaponless fighting techniques that employed the clenched fist as a formidable weapon. This later came to be known as *vajramushti* and was practiced by a warrior class called *kshatriya*. Also, in China, around the year 2674 B.C., the armies of the famous Yellow Emperor, Huang Ti, were reportedly well versed in a form of what is today known as Kung Fu, employing such recognizable fighting postures as the "tiger," the "grasshopper," the "monkey," and the "crane." By the time of the Feudal States, 770–480 B.C. (approximately the time of the Jewish captivity in Babylon), Kung Fu was already widely established and held in some measure of esteem for, according to the Book of Songs (*Shih Ching*): "Without boxing techniques a man is relegated to the lower ranks in the army." This quotation has been used by present day Kung Fu practitioners to illustrate that their system, which includes a style of boxing, was quite likely the first structured form of martial art, out of which developed all others. Obviously there's room for argument there, but little in the way of substantial evidence to prove otherwise.

Probably the first major influence in the development of the martial arts was exerted by Taoism. Founded by Lao Tzu in 600 B.C. as primarily a philosophy, it gradually evolved into a complex system of occult practices that included: contemplation, breathing exercises, techniques to insure health, and the search into the mysteries of medicine and alchemy. Many Taoists reportedly became skilled Kung Fu practitioners and were especially proficient in the use of swords.

But now legend and fact intermingle with blatant disregard for truth, and the singular object of these woven fantasies is the Buddhist monk Daruma Taishi or, depending on whose translation you read, Bodhidharma. Bodhidharma, it is conjectured, was a member of the *kshatriya* (warrior class) in southern India and therefore probably versed in *vajramushti*. During his time, about A.D. 520, he had received religious instruction in Mayhana Buddhism (known as Ch'an in Japan and, later, Zen Buddhism in the western world). It was a new religion, recently broken off from the traditional Hinduism and, perhaps because there was little in the way of local support for its foundation, Bodhidharma traveled to China.

The journey at that time was a long and treacherous one calling for a great deal of strength and endurance on the part of the traveler, not to mention some degree of self-defense skills to ward off the many bandits who plagued the trail much of the way. That Bodhidharma arrived safely at the capital of Liang Province is further reason to assume he was skilled in *vajramushti*.

Emperor Wu, who had heard tales of the monk's journey, initially requested him to teach him the tenets of his new religion, and ancient classics reconstruct a probable conversation between the holy man and him.

"I have built many temples and have had many of the holy books translated and copied. Have I not done much good?" the Emperor asked.

"You have done no good at all," Bodhidharma is said to have replied.

"What then is good?" the Emperor demanded.

"Purity and truth, depth and fulfillment," the holy man said. "Being wrapped in thought in the midst of stillness. These cannot be reached by building temples or translating books."

The Emperor, disturbed, no doubt, by the monk's opinion of his efforts, if not the complexities of his new religion, tired of him and soon the itinerant was on his way north to Honan Province where he reportedly took up residence at the Shaolin Temple in Sung Shan.

Bodhidharma himself was evidently highly proficient in the art of "being wrapped in thought in the midst of stillness," for he allegedly sat for nine years at the Temple facing a wall and meditating. Legend has it also that at one point during this period he unwittingly fell asleep and, upon waking, outraged at the thought of it possibly happening again, cut off his eyelids then and there. The next day he returned to the exact spot and discovered that two tiny shoots had sprung up from the ground where his eyelids had fallen!

Legend aside and some fact to the contrary, in between those bouts of endured meditation, Bodhidharma taught the Chinese monks the intricacies of Buddhism. His system, however, was apparently too rigid and his discipline too severe, for the student monks were unable to keep pace with him; they passed out from sheer exhaustion. In order to insure classroom attention, yet not compromise disciplinary tenets, Bodhidharma reputedly manufactured a system of exercises whereby the monks could improve both their physical and mental faculties. The aim of Buddhism, he is supposed to have told his students at Shaolin, is the salvation of the soul. But the soul and body being inseparable, the one suffers if the other is not of equal strength. If the body is in a weakened state due to the sedentary ways of monastic life, then the student might never perform the ascetic practices so necessary for the attainment of true spiritual enlightenment. And so Bodhidharma authored the *I-chin Sutra,* which later became the foundation for the Chinese system of empty-hand fighting. Bodhidharma apparently passed on some of the instructions he had received in *vajramushti* for, as time passed and the monks at Shaolin Temple studied and practiced the disciplines of the *I-chin Sutra,* they soon became famous for their incredible fighting abilities. Their system in China was known as Ch'uan Fa.

Ch'uan Fa (now called Kung Fu) is commonly broken down into two main schools: the Hard or External (Exoteric) Buddhist School, and the Soft or Internal (Esoteric) School of Taoism, and it is generally believed that it was introduced to Okinawa somewhere between the sixth and seventh centuries during the Sui Dynasty (about A.D. 560–618). At that time there was contact between China and the Ryukyu Islands (Okinawa is the main island) and there is good reason to assume that some degree of cultural exchange took place, Ch'uan Fa included.

According to Alexander Liu and Master Alan Lee, writing in the *International Martial Arts Convention Journal* in 1969, that cultural liaison "was increased greatly by the 14th century as Buddhist missionaries, immigrants and students travelled back and forth between the two countries, and the transmission [was] not limited to martial arts alone. The result was a fighting style that combined both Chinese and native elements. The art took on the name 'Tode' or 'Tang Shu' meaning 'Chinese Hand.' "

In the fifteenth century China's civil delegation to Okinawa was replaced by a military envoy, many of whom were proficient in a martial art known as Chinese Kempo, and the Okinawans readily adapted these techniques to their own system.

King Hashi then succeeded in unifying the Ryukyu Islands into a single kingdom, emphasizing sea trade, the fine arts, and, in order to ensure lawful rule, confiscated all weapons and made the mere possession of them a crime against the state.

Okinawa in 1609 then fell under the rule of the Satsuma clan of Kyushu of Japan, and for the second time the ban on all weapons was imposed. Those in possession of ''illegal'' arms were severely punished and as a direct result many instances of conflict and rebellion occurred between the resentful Okinawans and their Japanese overlords. The ban also served to unite the many separate martial arts schools that existed at the time, unifying and thus heightening the rapid development of a weaponless defense later to be known as Okinawa-te. ''Te'' translates to ''hand,'' and the term was eventually attached to the name of the town that practiced it, e.g. Shuri-te, Naha-te, and Tomari-te, three of the major styles that subsequently developed.

The Japanese, meanwhile, despite the secrecy guarding the martial arts movement, no doubt were learning and adapting the Okinawan styles with their own. But actual formal introduction of what we know as Karate didn't come until the twentieth century. In 1917 and again in 1922, Gichin Funakoshi, the man most responsible for the systemization and transmission of modern-day Karate, traveled from Okinawa to Japan under the auspices of the Ministry of Education, performing demonstrations of his ''new'' martial art style. Master Funakoshi, born in Shuri, Okinawa, in 1869, began his studies when he was only eleven with two of the foremost masters of his time: Ankoh Itosu of the Shuri-te style and Azato of the Naha-te style. Master Funakoshi learned his art well, merged what he considered the best of both styles and then formed what was later to be called Shotokan Ryu. ''Shoto,'' by the way, is the pseudonym Master Funakoshi used to sign his works of calligraphy. The word ''Shotokan,'' which was chosen by his students rather than himself, literally means ''Shoto's house'' or, more loosely, ''Shoto's school.'' ''Shotokan Ryu'' translates to ''the way of Shoto's school.''

Credit is also given to Gichin Funakoshi for changing the Chinese characters, which formed the word Karate, that had existed since the late nineteenth century. There were several changes in between, but his calligraphic style accurately reflected the Zen Buddhist philosophy of selfless strength. His characters were the symbols for ''empty hand,'' which translated to ''rendering oneself empty.'' The Okinawans began to recognize the character-building importance of Karate in the early 1900s, shedding their veil of secrecy and ultimately making it an integral part of the curriculum of the First Middle School of Okinawa.

Master Funakoshi also saw the spiritual aspects of the martial art, for he had written: ''As a mirror's polished surface reflects whatever stands before it, and a quiet valley carries even small sounds, so must the student of Karate render his mind empty of selfishness and wickedness in an effort to react appropriately toward anything he might encounter. This is the meaning of *kara,* or 'empty,' of Karate.''

Gichin Funakoshi stayed on in Japan lecturing and demonstrating to enthusiastic audiences, eventually opening his own school. And from this hub of learning came the hundreds of students, both Oriental and Occidental, who learned and later modified as did the master himself; they spread the basic tenets of Karate as Master Funakoshi wrote them, but introduced new angles, different techniques, created, ultimately, new styles.

By the middle of the twentieth century practically every country in the eastern hemisphere had its own form of martial art: Tae Kwon Do in Korea, Kung Fu in China, Karate in Okinawa and Japan. And beyond those a virtually endless list of varying styles, some with empty hands to others employing all manner of weapons: Judo, Jujitsu, T'ai Chi Ch'uan, Aikido, Kempo, etc.

American servicemen returning from active duty in the Far East after World War II brought home tales more wondrous than those of Marco Polo. Stories of incredible skills, superhuman abilities, iron fists, and banshee screams that changed mild-mannered men into powerful fighting machines abounded, and Americans listened intently.

Hawaii quickly became the stepping stone to the United States for Japanese, Okinawan, and Korean instructors. As the Chinese had adapted from the Indians, the Okinawans from the Chinese, the Japanese from the Okinawans, and all others from somebody before them, so, too, did the Americans eventually break rank with the Orientals and formulate their own style of Karate. Some called their system simply American-style Karate while others kept the original Oriental name but preceded it with the word Modified. There were dissensions, rivalries, guarded secrets, and open hostilities, much about which the average public was unaware. It wasn't until the early 1960s that the American public really became exposed to the martial arts.

It was only then that concerted efforts were made on the East and West coasts to promote tournament Karate. Up until then most of the intraschool fighting activities took place within a designated *dojo* (school); the public was seldom invited and little or no documentation was made of the results. But with the advent of ''open'' and ''invitational'' tournaments, these same activities were presented to curious and enthusiastic audiences nationwide. Public gathering places as small as someone's apartment and as large as Madison Square Garden in New York City were housing tournaments and exhibitions. Orientals and Occidentals competed with each other and borrowed a little from the other's style.

The northeast coast, New York, New Jersey, and Connecticut especially, was energetically active in promoting tournament competition. Likewise the West Coast. In 1964 at the International Karate Championships in Long Beach, California, Bruce Lee gave a demonstration. Attending that tournament was William Dozier, the man who had just recently created television's successful "Batman" series. He signed Lee to appear as Kato in his "Green Hornet" series. Kato captivated audiences everywhere with his back kicks, front chops, and assorted "flying" techniques.

Born in San Francisco but raised in Hong Kong, Lee was an occasional child actor and sometime student of Kung Fu. He returned to the United States and opened a Kung Fu academy in Seattle, Washington, when he was eighteen, and during the early 1960s opened two more in Oakland and Los Angeles. He made little financial headway, however, until the "Green Hornet" buzzed in with instant notoriety. When the series ended, Lee returned to Hong Kong to promote the dubbed version on Chinese television. During a much-publicized TV exhibition, Lee side-kicked five one-inch boards dangling unsupported in midair, breaking four of them and impressing film producer Raymond Chow. Chow quickly signed Lee to make *Fists of Fury,* an instant success, then *The Iron Hand,* a box-office bonanza that reportedly grossed more than a million dollars but only cost about $200,000 to make. Martial arts movies then began coming out of Hong Kong on a conveyor belt, all low-budget and nonartistic, but highly profitable.

The martial arts movement picked up momentum. The year 1972 saw the production of a TV movie called "Kung Fu," which starred David Carradine. Shortly thereafter it became a successful series.

In 1964 Japan introduced Judo to the Olympic games as its national sport, making it the first martial art to be included in these international competitions. For many years Karate has been under consideration as a potential candidate for the Olympics as well, but lack of standardization within the sport has been a major deterrent. While the popularity of Karate and the other martial arts continues to grow, there is no overall organization to govern rankings or styles. New systems led by self-appointed grand masters are constantly appearing with no one group having the least control over any of the others.

The growth of the martial arts the world over has been unique and exciting, yet not unlike the tree that labors long and hard within the gound, first gaining a root-hold, then shooting up tall and perhaps a bit precariously in its green youth. Time alone allows it to strengthen and mature. India and its aboriginal forms of Kung Fu might well be considered the root, while China with her modifications, embellishments, and ultimate establishment of the art would serve as the trunk. From that solid foundation branch off the respective and various styles of martial arts.

This book is designed to give the reader a basic understanding of the philosophy and techniques involved in the fundamental arts of T'ai Chi Ch'uan, Aikido, Judo, Karate, and Kung Fu. When followed faithfully, each of these arts yields very real and tangible benefits in terms of physical and mental well-being, as well as providing an effective means of self-defense. Yet each art is also distinct from all the others. Through this book the student can discover which form best suits his individual needs.

T'AI CHI CH'UAN

I. A PIECE OF THE PAST

Chang San-feng, known to his twelfth-century Sung Dynasty compatriots as ''the Immortal,'' sat early one afternoon meditating, just as he did every day for exactly six hours. Nothing diverted his attention; he was solidly locked in his thoughts. Suddenly, from outside the window, an odd sound erupted. Chang broke from his lotus position and walked to the portal.

In the garden below, head raised, was a snake, hissing at a crane in the branches of a nearby tree. The crane, after taking as much as it could from the bothersome snake, lifted its swordlike beak and swooped down. The snake moved its head slightly to the left, and as the crane grew closer, raised its tail and jabbed at the crane's neck. The crane lifted its right wing as protection against its attacker. Then the snake darted its fangs into the crane's legs, and the crane raised its left leg and lowered its left wing to ward off the stings. This went on for a few minutes, with the snake slithering away from its attacker, and the crane unable to make any solid contact. After a while the crane became exhausted, couldn't nab the twisting and bending snake, and flew back to its tree where it sat bleary-eyed, peeking over a wing at the snake who, just as tired, crawled into the tree trunk. The ritual was over for the day, but like clockwork the two of them would be at it the next day.

Chang watched the performance from his window for three weeks, and came to realize the value of yielding in the face of strength. He had been meditating on the *I Ching,* the Chinese Book of Changes, which states as its main principle the strong changing to the yielding and vice versa. Chang coupled the animals' movements with the environment they fought in—ground, air currents, the tree bending in the wind—and formulated a series of movements based on those he saw from his window. He called it T'ai Chi Ch'uan, a choreography of mind and body. That's the most popular version of how the softest of the martial arts began. But like all "original concepts" there are other accounts.

There was an Indian monk, Ta Mo, who supposedly invented his Shiao-liu exercise to bring his fellow brothers out of their degeneracy. Aside from the fact that the monastery was not functioning well at all—the monks slept most of the time—the men themselves, when they got up enough energy to walk around, could only move a few yards before falling down again. To alleviate the problem, Ta Mo, like a Marine drill sergeant, rousted them out of their stupor by assuming the attack position of some animals he'd studied. It was either fight back or get hurt, so the monks, as astonished as they were vulnerable, put up their hands to ward off their crazy brother. Finally, after a few months, the monks got the message and began doing their work. Ta Mo continued mimicking the animals and, soon, so did the other monks. What had started out as a means to motivate the brothers became a way of life for them.

The third "official" version had Hsu Hsuan-ping, a woodcutter whose etchings gave him inspiration, originate the Long Boxing Exercise, a series of movements containing forms of modern T'ai Chi Ch'uan: Single Whip, White Crane Spreads Wings, Step Forward, Seven Stars. The exercise, otherwise known as Long Kung Fu, added length and continuity to the philosophy of mental discipline and to the science of increasing physical endurance.

An example of the discipline needed to carry out Long Kung Fu—or any of the martial arts for that matter—is equivalent to the amount of concentration it would take to lift a car off someone trapped beneath it. What an ordinary man might be able to do in an emergency (jamming energy into every muscle in his body to get the car off), the practitioner of Long Kung Fu can do at any given time.

Yet another tale is associated with the dancelike movements found in T'ai Chi Ch'uan. In 2250 B.C. Emperor Yu ran into a problem that might have devastated his entire empire if he hadn't been a quick thinker. A flood contaminating his land with stagnant waters threatened to wipe out his country, so he ordered a series of exercises, which he called the Great Dances, to be performed by his people every day. If inactive waters become diseased, he reasoned, so do inactive bodies. The dances stimulated circulation in the people, and by implication started the water moving off the land. Yu's idea was far from original. Medical dances of a thousand years before prescribed specific movements for every disease in an effort to chase away the evil spirits.

II. THE LOWDOWN

T'ai Chi Ch'uan places the mind and body in harmony, and by its literal translation reveals its nature. "Ch'uan" means fist, metaphorically. Control is the main factor—control over one's own actions. T'ai Chi Ch'uan is the epitome of organized movement and at the same time the ultimate in self-protection. An expert in T'ai Chi Ch'uan has immunity from destructive external forces and poor health.

The idea of the fist takes on different meanings in the West and East. The Western man views the clenched fist as a weapon of destruction, aggressive attack, pounding the opponent into the ground. In the East it's more in line with concentration, an inner force generating tó the surface. The fist becomes separate from the rest of the body as the energy becomes concentrated in the fingers and hand. The Western "black power" sign is the perfect embodiment of strength and unification, and as such is closer to the Eastern concept than fist-as-killer in street fights or in the ring.

In T'ai Chi Ch'uan, "Ch'uan" means that the active is controlled by the inactive—the active is form and matter, the inactive, spirit and mind. The inactive control therefore places this particular martial art in the role of the softest of them all, the art in which the greatest amount of control is gained with the least physical effort. All life, according to this principle, has been set in motion by two vital energies: Yin, the passive, and Yang, the active, both of which feed off one another, complement each other. The motion or action in T'ai Chi Ch'uan is the Yang and the stationary or stillness is the Yin. They are always in perfect harmony.

The symbol, with Yin as the dark part and Yang the light, shows two small dots, indicating that one always lives in the other. The wavy line is motion, keeping the harmony forever flowing.

The movements in T'ai Chi Ch'uan, the Inner and Outer, are held together by the mental concentration necessary to reach harmony. The Inner Movement is of course the mind, one which is still and in the act of concentration. Quietness is the goal, and the *Chi,* the inner vital force, is reached when mind, breath, and sexual energy come together.

As the art of nourishment, T'ai Chi Ch'uan masters concentrate on inner breathing. The breathing itself, which should be done by taking long inhalations and then shorter exhalations, is practiced until a kind of heat is produced in the psychic center, found three inches below the navel. The heat, like vapor, is then given off and distributed to other parts of the body. It is essential to pinpoint the psychic center and feel its increasing store of energy. Then, after the heat reaches the limbs, the T'ai Chi Ch'uan player is propelled into action.

For the beginner it is advisable not to force the pace of abdominal breathing. The beginner should breathe in through his nose, slowly and in one relaxed draft, drawing the air deep within him, expanding the diaphragm and lower abdomen. Then he should exhale through the mouth, slowly, very slowly, until all the air is squeezed out by a steady but not forced contraction of the diaphragm. When the abdomen is finally relaxed, the Chi energy becomes active. It must be remembered that breathing as well as Chi is controlled by the mind.

One of the most baffling aspects of martial arts is "mind force," the principle of Chi, which states that a man who throws a punch with only brute force is not utilizing his full potential. By concentrating mentally on the punch, it is possible to deliver many times the force of the ordinary power punch.

The Outer Movement concentrates on smoothness and evenness; all movements should be executed at the same tempo and with total balance. The slightest loss of control breaks the pattern and interrupts the continuity. It disrupts the smoothness necessary for proper execution. With the body erect and in a central position, the player's body in an attitude of self-defense is like a bow and arrow, aiming directly at his target.

Along with the central position relaxation is necessary. The body acts as a series of electric impulses in T'ai Chi Ch'uan, but all movements are at the same energy level rather than any one part of the body being either more or less relaxed than another. In that way the action flows smoothly, each form following the previous one as if the player were engaged in a ballet. One movement flows naturally into the next.

T'ai Chi Ch'uan movements are always circular. When the player moves, his limbs rotate, without sharp turns or angles. The limbs are not the motivators of the movement; they are rather the transmitters of it. The mind is the motivator, the body the executor with all its parts working as a complete unit. When a player strikes with his fist, for instance, the energy is generated from his entire body in motion after the mind's command to act. The fist is the last part of the body to receive the initial instruction to act as it collides with its target. The T'ai Chi Ch'uan player knows that the impact will be far greater if he throws his body into the swing.

12

III. T'AI CHI CH'UAN TODAY

The Western man, because of his frenetic pace of living and generally superficial concern for his physical health, would do well to practice some of the movements of T'ai Chi Ch'uan. By taking a close look at everyday movements—walking to the bathroom, eating, scratching the face—an individual might begin doing these actions in slow motion, gracefully, watching his gestures, concentrating on their progress from one point to another. By slowing down the tempo he breaks up erratic patterns and tones down any restlessness. The result of this short but important exercise is that it alleviates tension and gives greater control over both himself and his environment.

Sophia Delza, in *T'ai Chi Ch'uan: An Ancient Way of Exercise to Achieve Health and Tranquility,* talks about five essential qualities used to crystallize the form and spirit of T'ai Chi Ch'uan: slowness, lightness, clarity, balance, and calmness. She says that slowness ''aids in the process of developing awareness,'' and by virtue of calm, deliberate movement a person accumulates a ''reservoir of energy.'' A person with a high, speedy metabolism, for instance, is often unable to focus it in one direction, but instead rushes, scattering energy. By decelerating and controlling the ensuing slowness, he will be able to find a direction, and in it act speedily.

Lightness, the second essential, enables a person to feel a continuity, a softness, regularity, evenness, a smoothness, and a flow in his actions. Instead of pulling or tugging against something, by allowing his energy to flow he will be able to, as Delza states, ''draw out the movement uninterruptedly from beginning to end.''

By slowing down and feeling the lightness, the third essential, clarity, will emanate naturally. Clarity enables the person to eliminate from his mind all extraneous thoughts. If, for instance, someone has to accomplish something in a hurry, he will be able to work much more quickly and efficiently with clarity than if he were bogged down with thoughts and ideas of no relevance to the subject at hand.

The fourth essential, balance, has to do with both the mind and body, with stationary and mobile equilibrium. T'ai Chi Ch'uan, unlike almost all other exercises, requires absolute balance at all times. When the body is in perfect balance there is no strain, no unnecessary constriction of muscles.

Delza says to achieve balance one must have: (1) physical ability, (2) an understanding of movement sequences, (3) an even flow of the movement and the control of the inactive, (4) control of the changes from Yin to Yang and from Solid (Shih) to Empty (Hsü), (5) control of movement from space to form, (6) mental awareness, and (7) a spirit of calmness.

13

The fifth essential, calmness, may be achieved by controlled breathing as discussed earlier. Or it may be achieved inductively as a result of practicing the other four essentials. Inversely, once calmness is mastered it then aids in obtaining mastery of the other four essentials. In the development and use of these five qualities a smooth and continuous whole is created in which the individual components of the exercise support and sustain one another.

One positive aspect of T'ai Chi Ch'uan has to do with health and cosmetics. The face, for instance, which ages faster than any other part of the body because of its constant exposure to the elements, often develops lines around the eyes and forehead. By slowing down the body and mind, and therefore not worrying about things as much, the aging process will be retarded and lines and other manifestations of aging will be deemphasized. By using the mind to first discover and then eliminate tension, the individual gradually causes the lines to fade from the face. The method may be called a kind of cosmetic behavioral psychology. By relaxing the face, by not grinding teeth or fretting from worry, the aging process continues at a normal rather than at an abnormal pace. Consider, for example, why there are so many martial arts teachers well into their eighties who look decades younger than their years. Daily practice of the five essentials—slowness, lightness, clarity, balance, and calmness—are the answer.

Women are treated with equal deference in the martial arts, and although few are presently engaged in the ''harder'' arts like Kung Fu and Karate, in T'ai Chi Ch'uan, which is essentially noncombatant, women, along with their male counterparts, find an inner strength and balance. Of all the arts, T'ai Chi Ch'uan is the most private experience. One needs no opponent to practice on; he practices on himself, developing his own psychic center and contributing to his own physical well-being.

Another positive aspect is posture. By practicing T'ai Chi Ch'uan, which requires an erect stance, the posture will gradually and naturally become upright. As the individual becomes more involved in the movements, he'll find in his daily routine that many of the T'ai Chi Ch'uan positions become more prevalent.

The best times to practice the forms are in the morning right after getting out of bed, which sets a high standard for the rest of the day, and just before going to bed, which in addition to keeping the muscles toned also encourages more restful sleep.

One of the most enticing aspects of practicing T'ai Chi Ch'uan is the absence of equipment and the need for very little space; an advanced student needs only four square feet. The modified short form of T'ai Chi Ch'uan is easy to learn. Its fifty forms take only ten to fifteen minutes to run through. (The long form has 108 forms and takes from between fifteen and twenty minutes.)

IV. THE HEALTH FACTOR

T'ai Chi Ch'uan differs from almost all other forms of exercise in that it focuses on all parts of the body simultaneously. Every muscle and joint harmonizes with natural and deep diaphragmatic breathing, which requires both tranquility and concentration to achieve success. Since the movements are in coordination with the mind, there's a beneficial effect on the central nervous system. It improves circulation, tones muscles, relaxes nerves, is reputed to have healed incurable diseases and chronic ailments such as hypertension, gastric disturbances, neurasthenia, heart disease, tuberculosis, premature ejaculation, and impotency.

Before going into the exercises it is necessary to eliminate all irrelevant thoughts, since the mind and not the body is the motivating force in T'ai Chi Ch'uan. It is also necessary to keep all movements flowing, each the natural extension of the preceding one, since equilibrium will be maintained through cerebral alertness.

One of the major mental diseases afflicting Western man is depression. T'ai Chi Ch'uan has been called the Eastern Evangelist as it diminishes depression, especially in the morning when the exercise day begins. Unlike other exercises that concentrate only on the body, T'ai Chi Ch'uan places a person in a harmonious duality of mind and body. If the outlook is promising to an individual, everything else will fall into place.

The effect on the heart and vascular system depends mostly on breathing properly, the single most important factor in T'ai Chi Ch'uan. Most masters have placed breathing ahead of all the postures, for it's in the lungs and diaphragm that the transition between the mind and limbs takes place. Deep breathing is directed by the mind to sink down to the hypogastric region during inhalation. "Quiet" breathing has to do with softness and slowness, and the person should fix an image of an artificial lung in his mind, as if he were actually watching the breathing itself. "Long" breathing simply means that the breath is taken to completion, without haste, naturally, like the body movements. The method of the Inner School of T'ai Chi Ch'uan places the Tan Tien, the psychic center in the individual, about three inches below the navel. It's to that spot that a person should try sending his breath.

Regulation or evenness is another important factor in breathing properly. When practiced, regulation of breath assists in cellular metabolism by indirectly influencing the even distribution of blood. Because of this, long periods of continual practice will not lead to fatigue. The effect on the digestive system of deep breathing is to provide exercise to the digestive organs and promote secretion of juices. This is true because all movement originates, via breathing, in the waist and abdomen.

15

Though T'ai Chi Ch'uan benefits sexual organs, the masters advocate temperance as part of their philosophical system. Sex, according to them, is very much what ancient biblical dogma dictated—for reproduction only.

Nevertheless, for the man not interested in saving himself, T'ai Chi Ch'uan has been known to cure nocturnal emission and premature ejaculation, as well as impotency. Since premature ejaculation and impotency are states of mind, and since the mind in T'ai Chi Ch'uan is the ruler over the body, through practice a man can use his powers of concentration to rid himself of these stigmas. Just as he concentrates on his breathing by eliminating extraneous thoughts, he may also concentrate on his sexual endeavors, without thoughts of his impotency interfering. It is no simple matter, but after concentrating his sexual energy on the act itself—and not on his feelings of impotency—the problem will be eliminated.

It is generally believed that a man should not engage in strenuous exercise within twenty-four hours after sex. The reason for that comes out of an ancient concept stating that the semen must be replenished before he can operate properly. T'ai Chi Ch'uan refutes this contention, saying that ejaculation makes way for fresh semen, a new source of energy. As the semen is restored the individual's power grows.

V. BEATING THEM SOFTLY

Observe a tennis match and see how each player carefully watches his opponent's move, and then watch how each player opens one moment and closes the next, looking for a weakness, a moment of imbalance, a small corner where he can slam the ball through. In all combat, whether it's in sports or on a battlefield, the adversaries jockey for position, trying to get the upper hand. But more than that, especially in T'ai Chi Ch'uan, each player watches for the opponent's strength, and uses it against him. It is not the impenetrable object versus the immovable force, but rather becoming sensitized to the opponent, that places an entirely different dimension on T'ai Chi Ch'uan.

Although much more spectacular, the "hard arts," such as Karate, are much less subtle. Attack is emphasized more than defense on many occasions, whereas in T'ai Chi Ch'uan the defense is the *modus operandi*.

The prime difference between the soft school of T'ai Chi Ch'uan and the harder schools is balance. T'ai Chi Ch'uan concentrates on balance to a point where the player is so proficient that he seldom loses it. In Karate, on the other hand, the training does not emphasize balance nearly as much. If the opponent falters even for a moment the adversary will drive home the winning blow.

Another significant difference between the hard and soft schools is the movement itself. The hard school puts its force in straight line power moves, while in the soft school circular motions are performed exclusively.

Hilda Brandt, an expert T'ai Chi Ch'uan player from England, once stood in the center of a room while two enormous men pulled on each of her arms, in different directions. After a moment, she simply moved her arms in a circular motion and spun the men to the floor. An even larger man from the audience didn't believe she could do it, so he and a friend demanded to take the same positions. They tugged and pulled on her arms for over five minutes. Ms. Brandt then looked at each one of them, nodded as if to tell them the time had come, and literally threw them against the walls on either side. The men, roughed up and astounded, left the room. They were back the next day to enroll in her class.

One of the most important differences between the two schools has to do with body action. The hard schools use the limbs as the main force center; everything emanates from the arms, feet, legs, and hands. When a match is going on, what the spectator sees are limbs flying back and forth. In T'ai Chi Ch'uan the entire body moves all at once, generating power from within and using the power by having it spring from the hand or foot. The hard school, in other words, answers force with force; the soft school uses the opponent's force against him.

Instead of meeting the opponent head on, in T'ai Chi Ch'uan the player moves away from the attacker, drawing his force from him and finally leaving him in a vulnerable position. It's almost as if the fist aimed at the T'ai Chi Ch'uan player is pulled from the arm socket, rendering the power ineffective. It's then that the T'ai Chi Ch'uan player moves in.

On the opposite side of "moving away" is "sticking," which occurs when the opponent himself is retreating. Instead of remaining stationary, the T'ai Chi Ch'uan player follows his opponent, copying his moves, until from exhaustion or confusion he corners him and soon after wins the match. "Moving away" and "sticking," as important as they are, would be useless unless the player follows the tempo of his opponent, matching step-by-step his movements and keeping time with them as well. If, for instance, the opponent throws a fist into the player's face, the player retreats at the same tempo that the fist is coming at him. If the timing is a split second off, the fist will either make contact or be just enough behind so that an extra surge will also make the same contact.

To understand force itself, the player must recognize not only its components in general but those characteristics of his opponent. His firmness, softness, speed, and direction take the seasoned player a matter of seconds to recognize. Before the actual combat the short period of time when the two men size one another up is like sparring, or—as T'ai Chi Ch'uan is often called—shadowboxing.

Quickness is essential to the expert player, and to achieve it the player must be in perfect balance at all times. He throws his fists or turns his body from positions of strength and not, as the losers find, from sudden thrusts or jerky motions.

In boxing, when the opponent attacks from the left, the player counters with a right. While the left side of the body absorbs the blow the player's right is attacking, using his body in a sweeping motion. As stated above, T'ai Chi Ch'uan is comprised of circular motions, so when the opponent attacks from one side, the player becomes a sphere, falling away on one side and attacking from the other.

In the Pushing Hand Exercise, the expert player will react to the slightest hit to the body, turn the opponent's strength against him and win the match. "Know thy enemy as well as thyself," said Sun Tze, a martial art strategist, "and thou would be invincible."

One significant aspect of the circular motion in T'ai Chi Ch'uan is that it has no beginning or end. When the player counters with a right the motion does not stop there, but rather, like a golf swing, the player carries through and proceeds to the next motion. T'ai Chi Ch'uan is a series of never-ending movements, meshing together, one after the next, until the exercise itself and the motion is over. Even when the player is stationary his psychic center is a bundle of activity, preparing for the inner motion to reach the surface. By standing in the center of a room completely still, the player first begins to envision the movement, the exterior ones, which will be fast coming on. It's almost as if there were a movie going on in the player's head before he sees the actual motion come to life in his body.

T'ai Chi Ch'uan is concerned with one of the most subtle manipulations of the opponent imaginable. The circular motions hypnotize the opponent, and like a man on his back looking up at a swinging pendant, the opponent sees the player's entire body become a human pivot moving before him. An eagle circling above waiting to sweep down on a rabbit, suggests calmness as it hovers silently in the air. A cat about to pounce on a mouse suggests alertness, both of which stun the opponent and hold him spellbound, making him an easy prey.

The image of the taut bow is what T'ai Chi Ch'uan players like to keep in mind when on the defense. The bow and arrow do not represent tenseness, but rather a steady watchful waiting, ready to spring. It's like storing strength, keeping it at bay until the right moment. The force itself is the arrow released from the hand, springing off the bow's cord straight at the opponent.

The difference between power that runs in a straight line and that which curves in toward the opponent, is the difference between the hard and soft versions of the martial arts. The straight away power has an end; it terminates when impact is made. In T'ai Chi Ch'uan, which uses circular force, the movement is never done, it moves right through the opponent and as it moves gathers strength for the next action.

The movements in T'ai Chi Ch'uan originate in the mind, and as such are not dependent on sheer strength. The player becomes selfless and utilizes the opponent's strength. When the spirit is calm, as it must be in T'ai Chi Ch'uan, the opponent's force is neutralized, putting him at a disadvantage. Extreme softness always prevails over extreme hardness.

In conversation, for example, the loud, overbearing man who tries to verbally beat down his opponent leaves himself open to the quiet, contemplative man who takes the adversary's arguments and logically disassembles them. While the loudmouth raves on, the quiet one is thinking, waiting to throw in a couple of sentences which more often than not demolish the arguments.

When the T'ai Chi Ch'uan player begins his motions they are large and exaggerated, and then, as the opponents grow closer to one another, they become smaller, more specialized, until, like short powerful jabs, they focus on vulnerable points. As the player improves his skill his movements are so small that they become almost unnoticeable. Appropriately, the movements have been called the "funnel approach."

The animal that best exemplifies the expert T'ai Chi Ch'uan player is the cat. Light, graceful, and stable, the cat moves in on his target with a lightning-quick attack, and then pulls back with the same speed and agility.

Exerting too much strength is the most common fault of the T'ai Chi Ch'uan beginner. It is important to remember that in T'ai Chi Ch'uan one should concentrate a smaller force in order to combat the opponent's larger force. Most strength exerted by the beginner is unnecessary, used at the wrong moment, thus depleting the energy level. Economy, in other words, is the key to conserving strength. Before each movement is made, there is a brief moment of contemplation—*thinking* about the movement itself. If the T'ai Chi Ch'uan beginner could visualize the movement before executing it, his strength would be concentrated only on those parts of the body that would be used. His mental control would naturally flow to his physical control.

The beginner has to be careful though. It is not often the most desirable thing to stand around thinking about what he does, especially when he must act immediately. The way to counteract this is to try concentrating on movements which do not require immediacy: for example, opening a door. It is a simple operation to turn the knob and pull, but by seeing the action in the mind's eye he will be able to use only that amount of energy necessary to complete the action. Furthermore, as time goes on, the mental concentration will become second nature to him. And when immediate action becomes necessary, the mental picture will be brought about subconsciously, automatically.

A second tendency, according to Lee Ying-arng in Edward Maisel's *Tai Chi for Health,* is speed. He says that the accepted notion that the faster man will be the winner is a misconception. Speed alone makes little difference in winning or losing; the ability to psyche out the opponent's quickness, his next move, holds equal importance.

Of major importance is the T'ai Chi Ch'uan player's ability to answer his opponent's reflexes with his own, to counter his movement spontaneously and immediately without thinking of the response itself. By slowing down, the beginner will be able to watch his opponent's moves and react to them without losing momentum or strength.

A third aspect of the beginner's training is evenness. Continuity of movement is essential in carrying out the action. With continuity comes graceful execution, a kind of ballet, in which the entire body moves all at once. Here the T'ai Chi Ch'uan player must be aware of his entire body. Any gap in one's actions gives his opponent the opportunity to penetrate his defenses.

It is often in the Western man's mind that slow, graceful movement should be reserved for women. Men, they think, should be tough, direct. Consider for a moment man's strength coupled with a flowing motion that carries his strength to his target with a force that he had never imagined. Consider also the fact that an evenness of motion allows one to control the situation he finds himself in. The idea of a moving target has always been appealing, especially to one who is on the defensive. By turning that concept around, by placing one's self on the offensive, the opponent must concentrate on his target—a target that is also on the attack.

A fourth preliminary for beginners has to do with roundness. T'ai Chi Ch'uan is a circle, and therefore all the movements are circular.

Lee Ying-arng, in *Tai Chi for Health,* makes this statement:

> If an opponent strikes me with a straight punch, his force is merely a straight line force. If I parry his arm and at the same time rotate my arm against his, this parry would be made more effective as this rotary movement of my arm is bound to cause the opponent to lose his balance. If the learner has any doubts, he could verify this fact on his friends. The art of Tai Chi, therefore, is the art of circular movements. These circular movements are performed by the hands, elbows, shoulders, chest, waist, knees, feet and by all the joints of the body.

Beginners should start their training by making larger circles than they think necessary. As they master the art the circles will become smaller, more concentrated, more effective.

The question of balance comes into play with what Lee and other T'ai Chi Ch'uan masters refer to as "double weightiness" and "single weightiness." By standing on the ground with one's weight evenly distributed over both feet and the center of gravity between them, double weightiness is in effect. The beginner who wants to move forward or backward must take all the weight off one foot and place it on the other. The problem with this is that in the meantime, while he is shifting the weight, the opponent can strike easily.

Double weightiness leads to single weightiness when all the weight is transferred to one foot. This can be clearly seen in the process of walking when there is a constant interchange of double and single weightiness. To guard against the unbalanced state caused by double and single weightiness, the beginner must always remember to keep weight distribution from not going outside a 20 percent area. If a person moves to his right, for instance, he must not let his right foot bear more than 60 percent of the weight for any longer than a brief second. The best way to practice this is to walk around the room, keeping in mind the 20 percent distribution.

We have already talked about breathing, but in line with the above mentioned preliminaries for the beginner it is necessary to reiterate Chi energy as it relates to the respiration.

As the beginner is conserving strength, contemplating his movements, slowing down his actions, making them more even and controlled, his breathing should coincide. As his movements are smooth and uninterrupted, so must be his breathing. It should above all be natural and unforced, as well as long and deep. He must concentrate on the air entering his body and then leaving it, and like watching a movie of his internal organs, he should be able to visualize the air moving to his psychic center where the Chi energy is stored. The mind in T'ai Chi Ch'uan is the controlling force; it manipulates the body, tells it that something may be wrong or deficient, so it must also be able to visualize what's going on inside. The air may be invisible to the eye, but not to the brain, not to the imagination. If it helps, think of the air passing into the lungs as a river emptying into the sea, liquid pouring into a glass, and then returning.

T'ai Chi Ch'uan manuals often refer to the body in terms of a tree. The feet act as the roots of the body's movements which are motivated by the thighs, controlled by the waist and manifested in the fingers. From feet to thighs to waist there should be unison in movements.

One of the wrong practices of the beginner is moving the lower extremities first and then the upper ones. It is essential to move them at the same time in T'ai Chi Ch'uan. By analogy, in a relay race, if the runner about to receive the baton were handed it while standing still, he would lose valuable distance and continuity. On the other hand, when he's in motion, a natural transfer takes place. Furthermore, by moving the lower limbs first, and then trying to follow through with a punch, the thrust and power of the fist will be nowhere near its potential. Harmony is the key to total body coordination, and is achieved only by the movement of one part accompanied by the movement of all.

William Chen, a master of T'ai Chi Ch'uan, shows in the following illustrations the fundamental moves of this graceful martial art.

BEGINNING

1. As demonstrated here by Master William Chen, the exercise starts from an erect stance with hands loose at the sides of the body. With his weight distributed evenly on each foot, he sinks slightly at the knees and raises his hands to shoulder level. By breathing slowly as these simple movements are executed it should seem as if the air itself were drawing the hands upward.

2. When Master Chen's hands reach shoulder height he straightens his fingers out a bit and draws his wrists toward the shoulders. To aid his concentration he stares straight ahead, fixing his eyes on a particular point. No extraneous thought should enter the mind. This is insured by concentrating on sending the air to the psychic center of the body, three inches below the navel where the Chi energy is stored.

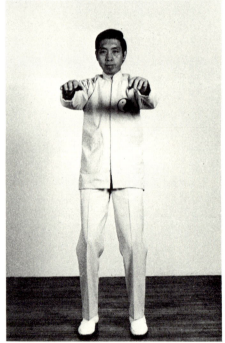

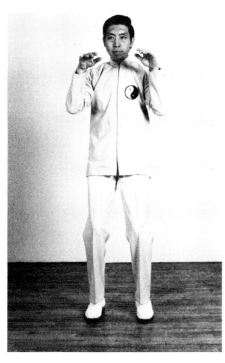

3. Notice how easily Master Chen moves, consciously avoiding becoming tense. He continues fluidly by drawing his arms toward the body, bending both elbows, and lifting both hands upward, away from his body.

4. Next, he moves his arms downward to the sides of the thighs. As he does this Master Chen keeps his wrists bent with palms facing the floor.

5. At the same time he bends his knees, keeping his back straight and the buttocks tucked in.

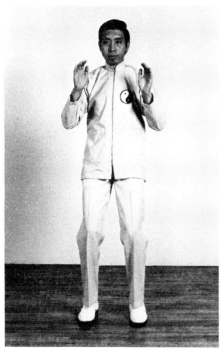

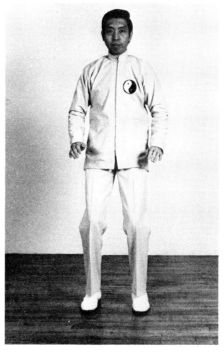

GRASP SPARROW'S TAIL

6. For this part of the exercise Master Chen reaches up with the left hand, palm inward, to take hold of the "sparrow's tail." With the knee straight he then moves his right leg outward and places the heel on the floor. Next, he transfers his weight to the right foot, bending the right knee and straightening the left. For this position, the body must always be in a diagonal line from head to left heel, buttocks tucked in and hips centered. Pictured here is a point midway to this stance.

7. The weight must then be shifted back to the left foot, while the left hand moves up to chin level, palm facing in. The right arm returns to the right side.

PUSH UP

8. Master Chen then pivots on his toes, shifting his weight back again to the right foot to obtain the stance shown here. Simultaneously, he raises his hands to just below chin level, placing his left fingers near the right pulse. The left wrist is straight and the arm curved.

PULL BACK

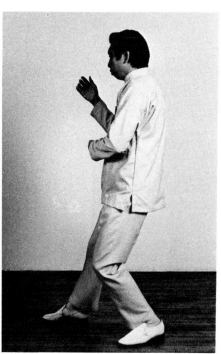

9. The weight is again on the left leg here. The right arm is brought up, palm facing left, while the left hand is brought close to the abdomen, palm facing in.

SINGLE WHIP

10. In this movement the left arm acts as a single whip, moving back and forth across the body. First the weight shifts to the left leg. The arms are slightly straightened.

11. Master Chen straightens his left knee and places his left foot parallel to the right foot. The left arm moves across the body, fingers pinched together, and the right hand comes to a point just below shoulder level. As the left leg moves over parallel with the right, the left arm moves in a circular motion across the body at waist level.

12. Master Chen then pivots on the left heel, turning his left foot 90 degrees to the left and bending the left knee slightly more than the right knee. His back is absolutely straight. As he moves his left foot, he turns his left palm to face northwest, fingers pointed upward. Both arms are now on the same level, with wrists bent. The right arm is extended out, slightly bent at the elbow.

PLAY THE GUITAR

13. In this instance the majority of the weight is on the left side as Master Chen pivots to the right on his right toes. His arms remain at almost the same height, left arm raised just a little. His left foot is pointed to the left, his right foot straight ahead. The palms are open, fingers apart. The weight is on the left foot, and the right foot is slightly raised off the floor—in playing the guitar the right foot is usually the tapping one, keeping time with the music.

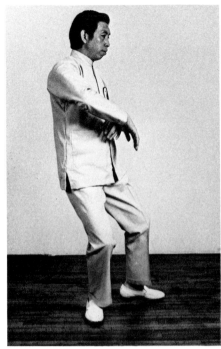

THE CRANE SPREADS ITS WINGS

14. Stepping forward with the right foot, Master Chen begins this maneuver. He drops his right hand just below waist level, palm inward, and brings his left hand up to the chest with the palm downward.

15. He continues by turning to the left, raising his right hand as the crane would do just before taking flight. The right hand begins a downward motion.

16. The right foot is stable on the ground while the left leg begins to rise. This position resembles the crane as it balances easily on one leg. The right hand moves to the forehead, palm open and facing downward. The knees are slightly bent. The movement is made with force and accent, in contrast to the previous exercises that were soft and graceful. The left arm here should feel as if it were pressing down on a hard surface, the right as if lifting a heavy weight.

FAIRY WEAVING AT SHUTTLE

17. Here the right arm is extended, wrist bent, and fingers of both hands pinched. Most of the weight is on the right foot, which is turned inward. The left foot faces straight ahead. The body is erect and the buttocks tightened.

18. Following through, Master Chen turns to the right and leans back on his left foot. His left arm moves across the body at waist level, while the right arm moves in the opposite direction to give the effect of embracing himself.

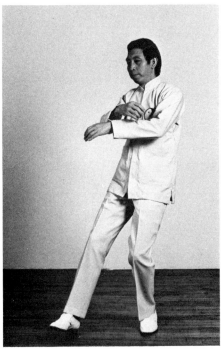

19. He continues turning to the right in a flowing motion, his head moving with the body and facing the same direction. The left toes are slightly raised off the ground, resembling movements at a shuttle.

20. Here the weight becomes evenly distributed, and the right arm, which had been tucked close to the waist, is brought forward in a protective gesture.

WAVE HANDS LIKE A CLOUD

21. In this case the circular movement of the hands resembles the swirling motion of a cloud passing in the sky. Master Chen begins by placing his weight on the right leg. The right hand is at chest level, palm down, the left hand rests at the waist with the palm up. The knees are bent.

22. With his weight still on the right foot and the hands in the original position, the body is turned a few degrees to the left. Master Chen's head is bent forward, his eyes focused on a spot on the ground ten to twelve feet in front of him for this maneuver.

23. As the body turns, the hands change position, the right hand dropping three inches below the waist, the left rising to the chest. The weight shifts from the left to the right side, and the knees are still slightly bent.

24. The image of the cloud continuing to move across the sky is maintained as the right arm drops lower and the left rises higher. Master Chen is positioned now over his left foot.

25. An imaginary wind now meets the cloud from the other direction. With his right heel raised off the ground, all of Master Chen's weight is placed on his left side. The body is in a position that would suggest trying to buck the force of the wind. The left elbow faces the ground, the right palm faces the left. The motion cannot continue as it had been going, and must be reversed at this point.

26. The body turns to the right and much of the weight now shifts to that side. The right foot is firmly planted on the ground, and the right hand begins to move upward while the left remains at shoulder level.

27. At this point the body has almost returned to its original place, except that now the weight is evenly distributed over both feet. Also, the right hand is extended further forward than at first, and the left is on an even plane with the right, just above chest level. The right foot is more forward than the left, which would give more balance against the strong wind.

BRUSH KNEE AND TWIST STEP

28. For this maneuver Master Chen maintains his weight on his right leg with his knee bent. The right arm is extended, wrist bent, palm open. The left arm is spread across the chest, palm facing in. The feet are pointing in essentially the same direction.

29. While bringing the right arm up, bent at the elbow, to a point a few inches above the shoulder, Master Chen lowers the left arm to below the waist and turns to the left. More weight is placed on the right foot.

30. The weight gradually shifts into a balanced position and the right arm is brought forward, palm still facing down. The left hand leaves the waist and begins a sweeping motion to the left.

31. The movement is complete when the body faces left, with the right arm extended in front, bent at the elbow, palm facing forward. At this point the left hand is just above the left knee and parallel to it. The weight is now on the left leg.

GET NEEDLE AT SEA BOTTOM

32. Here Master Chen lowers his hands to below the navel where the Chi energy is stored, as if touching the sea. Holding his hands straight, he continues lowering them until they reach the knees—the bottom of the sea. He shifts his weight from the left foot to the right by placing the remaining weight on the left toes. Lowering and relaxing his body he allows the palms to drop to the knees or just below, eventually placing the left hand over the right wrist, as if in prayer.

SINGLE WHIP

33. By pivoting on the right heel, Master Chen turns to the left, his arms extended and moving with the torso. With the left foot he takes a wide step forward and to the left, and then shifts his weight to that side. The right hand, pinched at the fingers, is held straight out to the right in a ready position in case it becomes necessary to strike. The left hand is in front of the face in order to ward off any blows.

SNAKE CREEPS DOWN

34. As Master Chen demonstrates here, the hand moves down to the foot as the entire body drops toward the ground. The motion, which imitates a snake ready to coil and strike, is smooth and serpentine. First pivoting on the right heel and shifting his weight to the right foot, Master Chen then pivots on the left foot and drops to a crouch. His arm remains in the single whip position. The left arm moves down along the calf toward the floor where it stays, palm facing inward, three or four inches from the ground.

GOLDEN PHEASANT STANDS ON ONE LEG

35. In this exercise, one leg and the corresponding arm are raised. When they are lowered the weight will then shift to that side of the body (in this case to the left). Whichever foot is on the ground while the other is raised must be pointed off to the side in order to get maximum balance. The foot in the air should face forward, at the target.

TURN AND STRIKE WITH HEEL

36. At this point the left heel is brought to the upper part of the inner right calf and the left arm is moved across the body below the waist with the palm turned toward the body. The right arm is moved down and out in a low diagonal. The right arm propels the body to the left and into a spin in the opposite direction. Shown here is the result of the turn. The move is particularly good for attacks from the rear. The left arm wards off the blow from the adversary while the left foot kicks him. The right arm is free to attack as well.

TURN AND STRIKE WITH HEEL

37. This kick is a circular one, taking its form from the round lotus leaves. From a standing position the left leg comes slightly forward and the right leg begins its high kick. The original position is 90 degrees away from that shown here. This position is the result of the body turning sharply to the left. The right arm has been sent across the body with the kick, adding momentum. The bent left knee will yield additional power when straightened out. Nearing completion of the kick here, the arms, which have been moving forward, reach toward the toes.

CROSS HANDS AND CONCLUDE

38. Before returning to the first position, Master Chen demonstrates the final movement. This gesture is at the same time a salute and an indication that the exercises are concluded.

AIKIDO

I. THE DISCOVERY

He stood just over five feet and weighed 165 pounds in his youth, and like the guy who gets sand kicked in his face by a Goliath beach boy, he decided it was time to make a man of himself. At the turn of the twentieth century, Morihei Uyeshiba, with his inheritance in his pocket and a need to get his body in shape, began traveling throughout Japan, seeking out teachers in the martial arts. With only a *bokken,* a wooden sword, in his hands he wandered through the country looking for a man better versed in the arts than he.

After becoming the most proficient man in all of Japan, he began to have doubts. He'd been taught that strength was the ultimate weapon, but after going through the trials and tribulations and the training he came to realize that strength was relative, that there was no absolute victory. "What's the use of controlling others," he thought, "when I can't control my own mind?" He put aside the martial arts and entered various temples to study philosophy and meditate. Continually he pondered the question: "What is martial art?"

One day, while out in his garden, the answer suddenly came, and Morihei Uyeshiba surrendered his already diminished ego and became one with the universe. "Golden vapor gushed out of the earth enveloping my body, and then I felt myself turning into a golden body. At the same time, my mind and body felt light; I could understand what the chirping birds were saying and I understood clearly the Creator's spirit. It was precisely at that moment that I received enlightenment: The fundamental principle of the martial arts is God's love and universal love. . . . Neither position, nor fame, nor honors, nor wealth, nor the desire to become more powerful than others have any attraction for me—these have all vanished.

"The martial arts are not concerned with brute force—to knock the opponents down—nor with lethal weapons to lead the world into destruction. The true martial arts, without struggling, regulate the *Ki* of the universe, guard the peace of the world, and produce and bring to maturity everything in Nature.

"Therefore, martial training is not training that has as its primary purpose the defeating of others, but practice of God's love within ourselves."

Professor Uyeshiba, says Koichi Tohei, the author of *What Is Aikido?*, "moves with grace as though he were performing a Japanese dance. . . . His every movement is in accord with the laws of Nature, and the power of the opponent who leaps at him goes back inevitably to the opponent himself. He has thus attained a state of absolute nonresistance."

II. THE PRINCIPLES OF AIKIDO

The universal energy, *Ki* (in T'ai Chi Ch'uan it's *Chi*), is at the center of Aikido, both in concept and in the name itself. Some call Ki God; others call it Buddha. Whatever the name, it is an energy flow which keeps the universe running smoothly, running at all. And man, as part of that universe, is composed of Ki, but in only a few of us has its expression approached its potential.

Aikido is one of the youngest of the martial arts—it originated with Professor Uyeshiba at the turn of the twentieth century—and it depends largely on the fusion of nature and physical acumen. It operates on the principle that spirit controls the body, but unlike T'ai Chi Ch'uan, which states that the spirit is refined before it is manifest in the physical, Aikido uses physical exercises as a way to get to the spirit.

Koichi Tohei, chief instructor at the General Headquarters Area of Aikido in Japan, makes these statements in his *What Is Aikido?*

> Aikido takes the leap from traditional physical arts to a spiritual martial art, from a relative martial art to an absolute art, from the aggressive, fighting martial arts to a spiritual martial art that seeks to abolish conflict.
>
> When the Aikido student is forced to meet an opponent he tries first to defeat his mind, for it's the mind that must be conquered before the body falls. In the Aikido match it's not conquering the enemy, but one's own mind. "Do not blame others nor hate them," say the ancients. "Be afraid only of your lack of security."

Strain is absent from the principles of Aikido; only obedience to the laws of nature is necessary. Let the opponent go where he wishes, let him return where he wants to return, and bend in the direction he wants to bend as you lead him, and then let him fall where he wants to fall. The Aikido discipline also states that what a person can accomplish by physical force is limited, what he can accomplish through nonviolence is limitless. In Aikido combat there is no practice in the use of brute force, but there is training in how to use the opponent's force against him. There is as much emphasis on training the mind and spirit in Aikido as there is in training the body. Just as a duality of mind and spirit has guided the great men through the centuries of civilization, the same principle applies in Aikido, the nonfighting martial art.

Aikido means literally the road (*do*) to a union (*ai*) with *ki,* the spirit, both universal and individual. The universal Ki is the real substance of the universe, from which all things come and all things live. Like the molecular fields that explain why we are solids in a flexible universe, Ki energy explains our spiritual conditions. Since the universal Ki inhabits all things, just as do God for Christians, Buddha for Buddhists, Allah for Moslems, there is inherent in the concept the warring factions of good and evil—the Yin and Yang, sunlight and shade, life and death—in the Orient. Sunlight and birth are positive Ki, death and destruction are negative.

The Aikido practitioner and teacher, therefore, are concerned with filling their environment with the positive and eliminating the negative. Plus Ki does not necessarily attack minus Ki in the Aikido training room; it replaces it. The training room is filled with plus Ki; the teacher sends it to the students who send it back again. Many students, even after a particularly trying day, take an hour or so on their way home to stop by the training room where they are infused with plus Ki.

What the student first learns in class is that, of all the martial arts, Aikido is most steeped in ceremony and ritual. While Judo, for instance, is a modern sport, the Aikido master, like the Zen master who discovers his place in the universe by shedding time and history and moving backward to his origins, also moves backward in time where ceremony and ritual determined his spirit. It is toward Aikido that many Karate, Judo, Kung Fu, and Jujitsu masters want someday to go. It is the most stylized and beautiful of the martial arts—it's been called a dance, a warrior's ballet. It's as active as gymnastics and as elegant and dramatic as Nureyev in *Swan Lake.*

The attraction to Aikido has more to do with precision and agility than with power and strength. The Aikido partners, for instance, work better together than those in the other martial arts. They are not in combat, not sparring with one another to see who will win, but rather they move around one another with a minimum of physical contact.

If it's physical fitness one wants, Aikido is the most appropriate of the martial arts as it concentrates mostly on holds and locks and not the attack-retreat aspects of Judo, Karate, and the others. Conversely, because Aikido is not based on self-defense tactics, it is the most difficult to learn. While the other martial arts might take two to five years to master (although one never completely masters them), most experts say five to fifteen years are necessary to learn Aikido.

It is ironic that the Aikido discipline teaches the correct principle of winning (that is, by first winning over ourselves) while at the same time shying away from the idea of defeating. One needs simply to succeed at whatever one does; the idea of having someone defeated is not taken into consideration. If someone loses a match, for instance, he is not considered the beaten one, but rather one who has won just as much experience and knowledge as his opponent. The Aikido person who is forced to defend himself against an attacker does not retaliate in the most vicious way. He is determined to inflict as little pain as possible on his attacker, and not, as some say of the other martial arts, to demolish him. It is more difficult to be gentle than deadly in combat, the reason why Aikido takes so much longer to perfect than the other martial arts. Those in Aikido are not out to defend themselves. Rather, they are concerned with developing their mental and physical natures.

III. AIKIDO AND EVERYDAY LIFE

In our everyday existence—eating, sleeping, the way we look, our subconscious—willpower is essential for our well-being. There are personal habits and practices we'd like to change, or at least modify, for better health. Through the use of willpower in Aikido this can be accomplished.

We will first be concerned with exercises performed during the course of the day, and later with more intricate positions best exemplified by photographs.

A Good Morning

When we awake in the morning the Ki energy is high, having been dormant throughout the night. Unfortunately, many people never get to sleep completely. A lot of people haven't had a deep sleep in years and have had to rely on eight hours of rustling through the sheets, worried about this or that, never really getting the profound sleep they sorely need. Those who have tried everything from drinking themselves into oblivion to reading a book eventually take pills, which do little more than offer temporary relief. The more they take the shorter their lives become. By applying Aikido, those same insomniacs can be asleep from within thirty seconds to a minute.

The simplest exercise, if practiced with regularity, has to do with Ki, located at the psychic center of the body, at a spot three inches below the navel, in the lower abdomen. Working on the same principle as counting sheep, the individual who concentrates on the spot for ten to fifteen minutes each night can, within just a few days, fall asleep instantly. Lie on your back with your arms and feet spread out and concentrate on the spot, and don't, like so many people, keep telling yourself that you can't possibly fall asleep. That's defeating yourself. By focusing on the spot, the blood rushes out of the head and toward the feet where it belongs.

It is also essential that the person must feel that if he can't sleep he may as well be awake. Why fight it? There's nothing worse than staying up all night determined to sleep when in reality there's no way to do it with that kind of attitude. Sooner or later sleep will come, simply because we all need it.

Concentrating on the single spot will eliminate all thoughts in one of the most effective ways possible. As you lie on your back with your feet and arms outstretched, breathe slowly through your nose, aiming the breath toward the psychic center. Consciously send the air down and feel it coursing through your body until it reaches the spot, and then push your blood further toward your feet. The head will cool off and the feet will get the blood they're supposed to. It should take about thirty minutes of the exercise the first time around. It seems easy on paper, but when you're actually involved in it your concentration must be absolute. If an extra thought or two sneaks in, apply more concentration until they're eliminated.

If sports teams use this breathing exercise to loosen themselves up, there's no reason why the average individual can't do the same thing. The results should be apparent within a few weeks: better performance on the job, a healthier look and outlook, and a lot more energy to take you through the day. There's also the extra added attraction of leaping out of bed in the morning, instead of lounging around in the blankets for a half hour or so, wondering if you should call in sick or not.

Getting Out of Bed

One of the most difficult tasks known to man is climbing out of bed in the morning. More excuses have been invented for not facing the day between six and eight A.M. "I don't feel good," is the most common. Or, "I had a bad night," or "I don't have *that* much to do today." All of which have little to do with the reality of a job or an appointment, but a lot to do with the actuality of pushing your feet over the bed and placing them on the floor.

Besides leaping from the bed the minute you wake up, a good cold bath will do a lot to spark up the morning. Even more invigorating than that is a solid hour of Aikido exercises each day before heading into the world. When the Ki energy is developed you become more mentally and physically prepared to act. Getting up in the morning is easier because a more restful night's sleep has been had and you will be eager to apply your reserve of energy to the day's tasks. What at first might seem like shock treatment will eventually become routine, especially when everything seems to fall into place at the office. The Ki energy will flow at a greater rate.

The Ki energy never lies dormant during the night; it flows through the body, is pushed in and out of the psychic center during breathing, and replenishes energy that was exhausted during the day. It also prepares you for rising in the morning. Willpower is the key in the initial stages, and the best way to accomplish the morning feats is not to think about them or anything else. Get up as soon as your eyes are open, run—don't walk—to the bathroom, throw cold water on your face. It's not only the exercises themselves that provide the positive feelings but also the *idea* that your life will become more active and interesting that propels you on.

IV. THE SUBCONSCIOUS

As far as Aikido is concerned with the subconscious, the breaking of bad habits sits high on the list of priorities. When someone knows for a fact that something he does is bad for him he usually has a hard time breaking away from it. For instance, smoking is obviously unhealthful, but because it's a habit, and a strong one at that, the individual has a twofold problem. In the first place, smoking is habitual, and secondly, he probably enjoys it. There have been methods by which some have terminated smoking—by eating an ashtray of ashes, for instance—but horror shows like that can be avoided by applying the principles of Aikido.

Some individuals conjure up myriad excuses to avoid confronting the real problem: "I was born that way"; "My grandfather and father did it, so it must be in the blood"; "My astrology chart says I'm inclined in that direction." In Western society the quick way out is most often the favorite way, or the only one that the person will pursue. But one must always remember that a step-by-step process is really the only way to accomplish anything. As in all things a certain amount of discipline is necessary to remove negative habits.

Bad habits do not only take the form of smoking or eating too much of the wrong things but many arise out of mental conditions—insecurity, egotism, and others. Suppose that you have been invited somewhere but you decide not to go because deep down you are generally afraid of meeting new people. On the other hand, you also know the party will be a good one that you should not miss. By throwing the blame on tiredness or disinterest you are masking the real reason, insecurity. Like getting out of bed in a hurry, the best way to overcome the insecurity is to go ahead with the original plans, go to the party, keeping in mind the fact that you will most likely have a good time. The Ki energy will flow at a greater rate, and any uneasiness you bear can be removed by breathing slowly and concentrating on the spot in the lower abdomen.

One of the best exercises is breathing deeply through the nose, sending the negative vibrations out and reinforcing the positive ones, sending them down to the psychic center. The Japanese are famous for their breathing exercises; they were originated to get rid of evil spirits, and anything inherently negative is evil. It's not just the great demons whom we must exorcise but the small ones as well. It might be beneficial to study some of the methods used by the ancients to rid themselves of these demons, and then apply the same techniques to remove personal ones.

The idea of changing negative thoughts to positive ones is one of the most important aspects of Aikido. It is not necessary to become a hermit and devote your time to contemplation to eliminate negative thoughts. Something simple like going out-of-doors or leaving a group of people for a few moments can be just as effective.

Anger, for instance, is a reaction to something or someone you disagree with. By becoming irate at another person you are adding fuel to his argument, encouraging him to continue with his line of thinking. Rather than banter back and forth take a deep breath and try to reason with him. If that does not work simply tell him you are no longer interested in continuing the discussion.

The ego, and the game of oneupmanship, prevents you from halting a heated argument. In Aikido, the ego is submerged, sublimated to reason. There is no reason to fight about something, especially when it isn't going anywhere. It becomes inconsequential wordplay, and any information you might derive from it is lost in the screaming match.

Many times the subconscious emerges in dreams, bad ones. To eliminate the nightmares practice breathing for fifteen minutes before going to sleep. That way, the Ki energy will locate itself in the lower abdomen and the dreams will be transformed from negative to positive ones. In the morning when you awaken you will be filled with an adequate supply of positive Ki.

One way to cultivate positive Ki is to look at yourself in the mirror immediately before going to bed at night. Stare at yourself, concentrating on restoring willpower and forceful character in your being—from thirty seconds to a minute. Focus on a single desire and tell yourself that it will be accomplished. After practicing for a while your confidence will emerge and the act will later be accomplished. After leaving the mirror go directly to sleep; during the night the positive Ki will grow until, by morning, the chances for success will be nearly 100 percent. Make sure, however, that you concentrate on one desire at a time. By thinking of a half-dozen or so wishes you will become confused, and instead of cultivating one wish you will spread yourself too thin.

The power of suggestion is most important in the mirror exercise. By looking at yourself in the mirror you are talking to the only person who can accomplish the mission. Many people lie in bed thinking about something they'd like to have, but they talk to no one in particular. The mirror makes you focus on self, the motivator of all your actions. This exercise also applies to habits: alcohol, smoking, stuttering, anything that afflicts one negatively. The exercise also, in an inverse way, applies to others who seek your advice. Rather than telling them that they have made a mistake, tell them instead ways they might correct their situations. Criticism can only be positive if results are offered rather than a reiteration of past deeds. For instance, if someone does something you particularly dislike, and he dislikes himself, inform him of the problem and offer suggestions to correct it. As a result the subconscious will emerge from burial beneath layers of impenetrable fears and phobias. With effort, bad habits, after their initial exposure, come to the surface, ready to be worked on.

V. TAKING THE PRESSURE OFF

People have often felt enormous pressure from their jobs and relationships, and often invent illnesses as excuses for not doing things, for not going outside their apartments and houses, for not living in a way they feel they should. The lack of control over one's nervous system is the prime reason for the emergence of the psychosomatic ills, especially in Western man, who feels he's in some sort of vise, applying constant pressure to him in his daily life. With so much confronting him he feels he must escape, and sickness is the best way—it evokes sympathy from others and literally takes him off the hook. He has by choice decided to live in negative Ki, complaining about his troubles to whomever he can find. Consequently, he has become a part of the national hypochondria pervading the country, and to alleviate his upset stomach, headache, and high tension nervous system he pops pill after pill. Like a sponge he absorbs not only his own problems but those of the world as well.

By working on the same principle that too much blood in the head causes constant turmoil and little sleep, the Aikido enthusiast concentrates on removing the blood from the brain and sending it toward his psychic center, to the point in the lower abdomen where positive Ki resides.

Some people, for instance, are so high-strung that even a small blemish will send them into frenzy. There is no logical reason for such erratic behavior over such a small item. The individual should instead concentrate on larger problems, for by focusing on the smaller ones he tends to carry over the negative Ki to whatever he confronts.

Ki energy, when properly used, affects every part of the body. Take the example of the man who can lift a chair by one leg. If he tenses his muscles it becomes almost impossible to lift it off the ground. Whereas if he concentrates on the hand doing the lifting, relaxing it at the same time, his chances for lifting it are much greater. He will lift it through sheer will, coupled with the strength derived from that will.

By stating right away that he cannot move the chair, he makes it impossible to accomplish the feat. Negative Ki at the outset makes it difficult to reverse the process, so immediately relinquish the negative for the positive Ki. If one has a positive reaction in the initial stages, the chair will rise from the ground almost effortlessly. What we are talking about is confidence, the kind that never wavers, never becomes frustrated. The fact that the chair may not be lifted immediately should not deter the man from continuing to try.

"The difference between a wise man and a mediocre man," according to Koichi Tohei, "is the difference between a man who uses an environment and one who lets his environment use him." Rather than pulling his forces together from within, the mediocre man allows, like a Candide figure, exterior forces to manipulate him. He loses self and becomes a composite of what others want him to be. That is not to say he loses his ego to them; rather he has no discipline, no individuality. He absorbs his environment until he becomes just like it.

The person who loses a lover, wife, or husband reacts to the loss according to what the society dictates. "I should feel this way about the loss," he says to himself, and stays with that interpretation, unhappy for much longer than he need be.

A young girl was left out in the cold by her lover. To keep herself from going crazy she repeated to herself: "I must forget him. I must forget him." There is no better way to keep a subject lingering in the mind than by concentrating on getting rid of it. It is far better to divert your attention to something else, a new interest. Some might say that thinking of something else is running away from the problem. Why? It is none other than severe masochism to dote on something which creates misery.

VI. THE PASSIVE AND ACTIVE

Many think that the passive and the active are polar opposites which never meet. In Aikido that is not true. As in Yin and Yang, the passive and active are in constant unity. The Aikido player is always in the zone between the two. The passive includes breathing, Zen meditation, thinking. The active has to do with playing sports, physical labor, gymnastics, practicing the martial arts. Those who engage solely in one or the other eventually find that they are deprived of an essential force in their lives.

We have all seen people who spend the majority of their time sitting, intellectualizing, sleeping. For them, mental activity is all that counts. They grow fat, lethargic, physically impotent. They become ashamed of their bodies, and the larger they grow the more physically inhibited they become. If such a person is bright he often uses his intelligence as a shield against his physical ineptitude.

The frantic, overly active individual, on the other hand, who uses his body without thought of passivity lacks unity. Aikido allows the active and passive to fuse together, pulling the best aspects from each. Both the active and passive are born of Ki energy; one state implies the existence of the other. Violent activity, for instance, implies calmness.

The man who rushes to catch a bus or who must dress in a hurry to make an important meeting, by remaining calm and consciously in control of his actions will be able to accomplish what he has to more easily and with greater expedition. So it is in Aikido combat. Against four or five opponents, the Aikido player must be aware of his adversary's actions. All of them. If he were to break from the calmness, even for a moment, his chances for losing would be four or five times greater.

VII. BEGINNING

The worn-out saying that an old dog can't learn new tricks does not apply in Aikido. The beginner, whether he's old or young, must learn to admit to himself that what he's previously been told can be altered or enhanced.

Frankness, for example, is not only concerned with telling the truth to others. It also applies to telling one's self. Many people, because they have accepted certain things during their lives, are not willing to have their minds changed. Through the years they have accumulated data that has fortified their beliefs, especially in things they can or cannot do. Through Aikido their universes are expanded. Opportunities arise that they have long since decided were too difficult, too far out of reach. Admitting to one's self that an action can be accomplished is one of the major facets in the experience of Aikido. By shaving away preconceived notions the beginner will have a world of opportunities open to him.

In *Aikido in Daily Life,* Koichi Tohei tells of a woman teacher who asked him to explain what Aikido was all about:

I explained the idea that the spirit controls the body and the principle of the unbendable arm. I then had her tense her arm as much as possible, and I bent it. She said, "You can bend my arm because you are strong and I am weak." "Very well," I said. "This time do not tense your arm, but think with all your being that your own spirit's strength is flowing out a thousand miles ahead." She seemed to be doing as I asked, but I could still bend her arm. Since further explanation would have been useless, I asked another woman standing by to help us. I asked her first to tense her arm. She did, and the woman teacher was able to bend it. Next I asked our new assistant to relax her arm and to concentrate on her spiritual strength flying forward a thousand miles. I then had the teacher try to bend her arm, but she could not. The second woman said, "This is wonderful, I understand exactly." The teacher insisted that she could not bend the other woman's arm because the other woman was stronger, though in fact the teacher was the larger of the two. I said that the teacher had been able to bend her arm when she had tensed it, and the teacher replied, "She let me bend it on purpose." Though the second woman denied that this was true, the teacher stubbornly refused to believe her. I saw no sense in explaining further. If the conversation had been in Japanese I might have gone on, but my poor English was not up to the task.

Tohei's point is that one must first believe in order to accomplish. By remaining adamantly against the notion that the second woman played a trick on her she was at the same time playing a trick on herself. By that one incident, the teacher viewed the wonders of Aikido as trickery and chose not to have her original question answered. If, however, she at least entertained the notion she would have discovered myriad sensations and mysteries that Aikido had to offer.

Learning Aikido is the unfolding of knowledge. You are exposed to it little by little until you are gradually aware that your senses and body are becoming harmonious, complementing one another. Too many individuals, whether they know it or not, are operating with a severed head. The mind has been cut off from the body, leaving the two operating on entirely different levels. What Aikido tries to accomplish is a unity between the two, to make them one, a single unit functioning for the betterment of the person.

Most Aikido masters say that one year is the amount of time needed for a basic introduction to Aikido. When a person first enters an Aikido school the master will look at him, and according to age, temperament, and enthusiasm the teacher will set a training program. The results in terms of physical and mental well-being will generally be the same, only the paths will differ for each student. The beauty of Aikido, as well as the other martial arts, is that there is no one prescribed formula or strict schedule to which a student must adhere. There is no competition among students to excel; the goal instead is for personal satisfaction. Since this is the case, each individual progresses at the pace best suited for him, under the guidance of his instructor.

In the following illustrations, Y. Yamada demonstrates the basic movements found in Aikido. Mr. Yamada came to this country in 1964 and since then has become head instructor at the New York Aikikai and chief instructor and president of the United States Aikido Federation. With him in these illustrations are three of his students: Harvey Koningsberg, Jenny Worsnopp, and Andy Worsnopp.

WARM-UP EXERCISES

LEG STRETCHES

1. Master Yamada demonstrates the first of these exercises, one that stretches the thighs and legs. By placing the left foot flat on the floor he is able to extend the right leg to the right, heel to the floor, toe pointed up.

2. This is the same exercise, except that this time the right hand is placed on the right knee and pressed down for a count of ten. The hand is then released and the exercise repeated.

SHIFTING BALANCE

3. Master Yamada begins this exercise on his rear foot and starts forward, keeping his arms in front of his body at all times.

4. Following through, the weight is moved forward to the left foot, and the hands, which were balled before, are opened. Opening the hands makes going into an attack from this position possible. The exercise is designed to develop better balance.

FRONT FALL
(Ukemi)

5. In addition to alleviating a fear of falling, this technique can throw the opponent off-balance. The Aikido fall is not only cushioning or breaking the impact but is also a defensive maneuver. The result of the fall will put the defender in a position to come back on the attack. Here the middle of the technique is shown. The fall is off to the side, creating a rolling effect.

6. Master Yamada illustrates here how to react when thrown backward to the ground. First, he simply falls backward with the momentum in order to regain his balance.

7. As soon as he can he then grabs his left leg under the knee with both hands and pulls himself forward.

8. His right leg, curling beneath the left, will add leverage in trying to stand up.

9. The momentum gathered while rolling forward should enable the person on the ground to rise quickly to his feet again.

KATATE TORI SHIHO NAGE
(Irimi Movement)

10. In the Irimi ("entering") movement, the defender moves toward the attacker. At the outset, Harvey, as the attacker or *Uke,* grabs Jenny's left wrist. Jenny, the defender or *Nage,* should point the fingers of her left hand in the direction she intends to move and at the same time extend her Ki, universal life energy.

11. Jenny moves to Harvey's side, away from his power, and starts to grab his wrist to pull him toward her.

12. Applying pressure to Harvey's wrist as she pulls him, Jenny is able to release her left hand from his grip. She puts her left foot forward and brings both arms upward so that she has enough space to pivot (her next movement, not shown). If the arm is too low, she will not be able to hold his wrist easily.

13. Jenny takes one step back with her left foot and grabs hold of Harvey's wrist with both hands. Keeping her body low, knees bent slightly, she twists his wrist so that he swings 180 degrees as she herself pivots and then locks his wrist behind him. Her hands still point in the direction she intends to throw him.

14. By pulling down on his arm, both hands on his wrist, she pushes him toward the floor. Her left foot is still extended in front of the right.

15. Since her feet are spread apart, Jenny has the balance she needs to hold Harvey to the floor. She has maintained her grip on his wrist with her right hand. Throwing him backward to avoid pain, Jenny has used Harvey's strength against him and gained control of the situation.

KATATE TORI KOKUY NAGE
(Grab to wrist)

16. In this first illustration Master Yamada has his arm grabbed by Harvey. When Harvey attacks, Master Yamada does not try to stop his movement. Instead, he pulls Harvey in the same direction, and the attacker's energy is transferred to the defender. Timing is important here, especially when Master Yamada allows Harvey to continue his motion. He must know the exact point at which to begin using his own power to throw Harvey off-balance.

17. Master Yamada gains the initiative. He extends his right arm skyward. Harvey loses his balance because he is holding Master Yamada's arm too tightly and all his power is concentrated on it. Master Yamada will lead Harvey to the right while he brings his own left foot forward.

18. Master Yamada has caused Harvey to lose his balance by trying to pull him high off the ground and to his rear. He has returned Harvey's momentum (which he took from him in the previous illustration) and is about to successfully use it against him.

19. With his opponent off-balance, falling to the rear, Master Yamada continues throwing his arm back, gliding with the opponent's motion. The completion of the maneuver has Master Yamada flipping his opponent to the ground, as shown here.

TENCHI NAGE
(Heaven and Earth)

20. This is another throwing technique that utilizes the opponent's strength against him in a backward direction. Master Yamada, the defender, has one arm pointed up, the other down—thus the heaven and earth. Both hands are in motion as he steps in toward his opponent at an angle, trying to throw him off-balance.

21. Master Yamada extends both hands so that the opponent will have to follow. This is also a defensive technique, with the defender trying to ward off the attack.

22. Moving his right foot forward, Master Yamada throws his opponent further off-balance. Harvey's grip is loosened on Master Yamada's right arm, while the left remains loosely on Master Yamada's wrist.

23. Here Master Yamada pushes. both arms downward to the floor where he wishes to drop the opponent. For this move the Ki energy must flow in the direction the opponent is to fall.

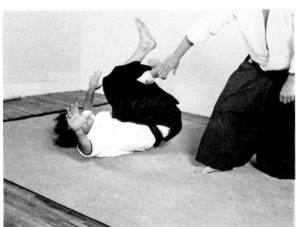

USHIRO KATATORI
(Grabbing shoulder from behind)

NIKYO
(Twisting wrist)

24. Harvey, again the attacker, grabs Jenny's shoulders from the rear, and she readies herself for a counteroffensive.

25. Sinking down, Jenny pulls the attacker with her.

26. She then ducks under his left arm, and when her right knee hits the floor she places her right arm on his left wrist. Her right hand goes to his left elbow.

27. As the attacker is thrown off-balance, Jenny rises to both feet and, by applying pressure to his elbow, forces the attacker to the floor.

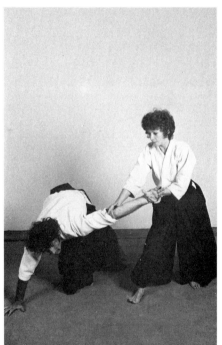

28. Once the attacker is on the floor, she bends down and puts an armlock on him. In this position he has no chance to retaliate.

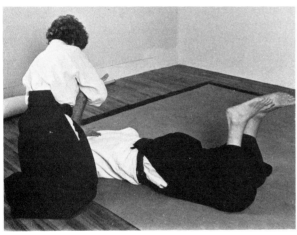

29. In this final illustration Jenny has taken hold of the attacker's wrist and has also extended her left hand across his elbow. If he makes a move to get up she will break his arm at the elbow.

SHOMEN UCHI
SANKYO IRIMI
(Blow to the forehead)

30. The Sankyo technique is a basic "lock" which is extremely painful and can be used effectively in self-defense. Here opponent Harvey attempts to strike Master Yamada with his right hand. Master Yamada grasps the opponent's wrist with his right hand while putting a lock on his elbow with his left.

31. By moving to the side and letting the opponent continue moving in his original direction, the defender is able to begin throwing him off-balance. Master Yamada continues to defend himself against the attack with his right hand, while his left hand is on Harvey's right elbow.

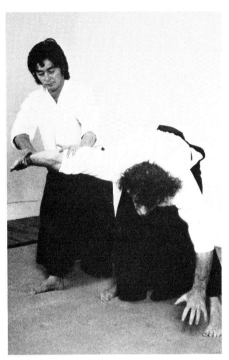

32. As the opponent begins falling toward the floor, Master Yamada pushes him in that direction. In order to ward off any opponent in Aikido it is necessary to allow him to continue his motion. By pulling up on the opponent's wrist and pushing down on his elbow, the defender is able to lock him in.

33. The conclusion of the technique shows Master Yamada with the same grip. As the opponent falls to the floor, Master Yamada continues with him, holding his arm against the surface in an effort to keep the opponent from staging a comeback.

SHOMEN UCHI
KOKYU NAGE
(Front strike)

34. Harvey, the attacker, will attempt to hit Master Yamada with his right fist. Here both men face each other.

35. As Harvey comes in, the defender moves to his left while extending his right arm away from his body to the right, keeping it straight. By sidestepping his opponent, Master Yamada is able to move into an advantageous position.

36. Master Yamada's right arm sweeps up and wraps itself around the opponent's neck, while his left arm curls behind the opponent's neck.

37. By moving to his left, Master Yamada is now able to pull his opponent in his own direction. He then throws the opponent off-balance and pushes him to the floor.

KOKYU NAGE
(with two people)

38. Kokyu Nage involves primarily throwing techniques that do not apply pressure to any joint. Strong Ki energy, fine timing, and good balance are a must. Here two men simultaneously push and pull Master Yamada. It is impossible to flow with both men's movement since they are attacking from different directions.

39. Master Yamada moves to his right, his strong side, attempting to break the hold of the opponent on that side.

40. He then sweeps under that opponent while pulling the opponent on his left.

,

41. Spreading his feet wide as he brings the two opponents together, Master Yamada moves his right arm up to their necks and begins pushing them off-balance to the rear. Once they lose balance, they begin falling backward. This is the chance the defender has been preparing for. He uses their backward motion to his advantage and continues with them.

42. By using his left arm as additional leverage he continues to throw them back until they fall to the floor.

JUDO

I. ART AND HISTORY

In 1882 Jigoro Kano, a student of Jujitsu, felt that his art lacked something. He put aside his training in an attempt to discover a spiritual meaning behind the combat he had been practicing for most of his life. Kano saw that mental as well as physical training was important in order to develop the person in a complete way. He also saw the need for a Japanese national sport, something that the average citizen could practice. Today, because of the practicality of Judo and its availability to all people, it is the most practiced of all the martial arts. It was originally conceived, according to G. R. Gleeson in *Judo for the West,* "to fill a gap in the physical, recreational and educational requirements of a people needing to play purposefully and beneficially."

Judo as an art is the method of arriving at self-realization and true self-expression; it is a science because it implies a mastery of various laws of nature: gravity, friction, momentum, velocity, weight transmission, and unison of forces—a realization of the spiritual sense of self in the philosophical rather than religious sense of the word. By illustration, we can see how a combination of the physical and spiritual senses may be applied to a person's makeup.

Miyamoto Musashi, a master fencer, sat one day on his small flowered bench and watched his student approach. It was early in the afternoon on that summer day seven centuries ago. The Japanese pagodas, small, beautifully colored relaxation and prayer huts, stood like soldiers in the background, their blue and amber roofs glistening in the sun. The student walked slowly toward the master, bowed, and waited for the old man to speak.

"If the mind is as clear as the mirror," Musashi said quietly, raising a finger to his snow white hair, "there is no use for a sword."

The student bowed and left. A few moments later he returned, this time from the rear, with a dagger in his hand. He crept slowly toward the master who was still meditating on his bench. Just as the student was about to plunge the dagger into Musashi, as a test of the master's skill, the master leaned forward slightly and pulled the corner of the mat on which the student stood. The student toppled over. The master turned to his disciple and with a smile said, "And what are you doing?"

The point of the story has to do with the development of mental and physical discipline to such a degree that one can control his environment; the master's mind was so tuned to hearing the slightest movement, so free from extraneous thoughts, that he was able to retaliate before actually being attacked. Like the other martial arts, Judo teaches one to anticipate, to perfect his senses to a point where he is able to defend against any attacker before the attacker can strike. Yet, in order to strike back, the Judo player's mind must be developed as a kind of warning system to hear the enemy approaching.

In one sense Judo can be defined as the study of the maximum use of the body and the mind for the purpose of attack and defense. In a larger sense the principles of Judo can be applied to everyday life: it develops the body, provides skill in combat, and develops mental and moral attitudes.

Philosophically, the true value of any art form, whether it's in music, writing, sculpture, or Judo, is the discovery and development of the potential within the artist himself. In the combative arts the artist is challenged to outdo both his own and his opponent's speed, physical superiority, and mental alertness. In Judo, the first and most important of these is to develop mental superiority. The artist who has achieved serenity of mind is able to concentrate on what he and his opponent are doing and is thus in control of any situation. Calm and assured, he will respond by conditioned reflex to an attack with accuracy.

Jiichi Watanabe and Lindy Avakian, in *The Secrets of Judo,* talk about the effect of Zen on the Western Judoist.

> There seems to be no serious reason for the Western judoist to adopt this practice, since the Zen effect is embodied in the exercises of judo itself: exercises that require the student to re-enact the Zen performance in its adaptation to practical techniques. During free exercise, which is similar to sparring in boxing, one learns to give way "softly" to the quick movement of the opponent. These exercises also serve to train the student in adaptation to continual change. They are called *kata,* and their purpose is to teach the principles of judo.

73

Self-defense is only one aspect of Judo. The nucleus must always be mental control. We must also realize that even though Zen is founded on religious beliefs, the philosophy behind it can be applied to both social and personal inclinations.

The average person, even though his goal may not be to master the art of Judo, can find enjoyment in its basic phases, as a mental or physical culture, as a sport, or as a means of protecting himself in the art of self-defense. The results of such training will in all cases develop a healthier body, greater physical control and balance, and increased alertness. Judo is no longer reserved for those interested in spending years training in dojos, or classrooms, but rather can be practiced by people of all ages and both sexes.

Judo has been called "the natural art," devoid of mystery and danger. This is not altogether true. The mystery has much to do with the discovery process, the unfolding of parts of one's body and mind that have remained dormant for years. One of the main reasons why many persist in the exercises is the wonderment, the curiosity of what might emerge.

The danger can come from any number of directions, most of which are based on the fact that the Judo player has not taken sufficient time or dedication in the art. Remembering that serenity of mind is the ultimate state in which the player can master his art, it does no good to hurry through Judo. Unless the basic techniques are learned, the more advanced ones will be almost impossible to grasp. For example, if one does not learn how to fall properly, he could conceivably break his back.

Because Judo does not allow rigid, set movements—the system harmonizes one's movements with the opponent's brute force to gain victory—the subconscious mind is trained to react to everyday experiences in a flexible manner. Say, for instance, that one is attacked by a prizefighter who, by the nature of his own art, uses brute force to down his foe. The prizefighter, like the Judo player, knows where his opponent's vulnerable points are, but, unlike the player, his mental exercises have not been as emphasized. His is not the subtle fighting of the accomplished Judo expert, and thus he calls up his powers primarily from his body.

It has always been a favorite topic of conjecture whether a top prizefighter or a Judo expert would win a contest against one another. Because each would certainly have powerful bodies ready to attack or defend at will, the question of force is not important. What matters is the mental training. The fighter trains for his next fight; the Judo player trains for the next moment. For example, why are there no prizefighters in actual competition over the age of fifty, and few over thirty? And why, on the other end of the spectrum, are there so many martial arts experts in their late sixties and seventies still practicing? Undoubtedly, it is the mental and spiritual training of Judo, in addition to the physical exercise, that enriches and strengthens their lives.

II. JUDO DYNAMICS APPLIED

Reaction time, the moment between the action and the reaction, figures significantly in Judo. Reaction time is lessened by the exercises, some of which are shown later in this chapter. The more repetitions you do each session the greater your speed and agility become. The cases when reaction time becomes longer are:

1. When one is not trained in Judo. No matter how proficient one may be in the art of self-defense, if he does not practice his exercises with any regularity his timing will be off. The length of a Judo student's reaction time after his opponent has struck determines who will gain control of the situation in the next move. Practice of the basic technique alone until it is mastered perfectly yields the ability to respond quickly and accurately.

2. When one's body and mind are fatigued. Again, practicing the exercises with regularity is a must. With faithful practice the beginning Judo student will find he tires less easily since his muscles are more firmly developed and he is in better, more alert, mental and physical condition.

3. When one is absentminded. Concentration plays an essential part in Judo, whether it's in actual combat or in the sport fighting and sparring. When you watch your opponent your eyes should not be moving back and forth from one part of his body to another. Instead, focus on his neck. From that point you will be able to see what all parts of his body are doing. Your mind will register his movement and you will be able to react accordingly.

4. When one is emotionally upset. It obviously does no good to enter combat or sparring with problems on your mind. A series of breathing and physical exercises before the match will temporarily eliminate the problems. Often, when a Judo player has not warmed up sufficiently before a match his reflexes will suffer and his chances for winning will be almost nonexistent. Your opponent, even though he may not be trained in Judo, will recognize these weaknesses and exploit them.

The following are methods by which you can lengthen your opponent's reaction time:

1. During a match, if you find your opponent focusing too strongly on each individual movement you make, embellish your movements—make them larger. When he reacts to the extraneous, larger movements, which disguise the smaller, more concentrated attack you are preparing, you will have the opportunity to strike more quickly and with greater effectiveness.

2. When your opponent realizes that you are capable of utilizing a striking technique from both sides, his concentration will be divided and, consequently, his reaction time will double. By capitalizing on your opponent's weakness—his divided attention and longer reaction time—he can be thrown off-balance and a successful strike against him can be executed.

3. Indirect sight figures importantly in sparring with the opponent. When he focuses on one part of your body, the part he thinks you are strongest at, attack from the other side. What he cannot see directly, cannot be effectively guarded against.

4. When your opponent inhales, his reaction time is longer than when he exhales. We exert a stronger force when we exhale. When releasing breath, we also release energy in the direction of the opponent. When we inhale, we pull the power into ourselves. The reaction time, therefore, is lengthened.

5. When you see your opponent go slightly off-balance his reaction time is longer. After a strike that misses, for instance, he is most vulnerable. In that moment of trying to regain composure he is less able to ward off one of your blows.

In the practice of Judo it is essential to understand the concept that it takes time to move a solid object. Certain parts of the body take more time to move than others. The hands and feet, since they are more mobile, move more quickly than the waist and upper torso. Posture, then, is essential to good defense. In order to throw the opponent you must take him off-balance, especially his torso, which will take longer to get back into the correct position. It usually takes from between a quarter to a half-second to get into a defensive posture; in that split second the body is unguarded. Look carefully at your opponent's movement and harmonize with it—fall back when he moves forward and vice versa, and remain calm at all times. Sudden jerky movements give him an opportunity to move in for the kill.

In a philosophical way you must become one with your opponent, as if you are both on opposite ends of a seesaw. His motion becomes your own as you jockey for position. When he pulls you toward him, apply force and actually push him further than he intends to go, thus knocking him off-balance. By absorbing both his and your own force you can turn it all against him and win. Before beginning practice, however, there are certain tips you must follow, for safety.

Only the most experienced Judo players can be thrown on hard surfaces, so for the beginner a mat is essential. But if a mat is not around, any soft surface will do—grass, shag rugs, sand (without shells or rocks), sawdust. It is always best to practice with someone who is better than you; that way the contest will not turn into a free-for-all, most likely ending in someone getting hurt.

If one or the other feels pain and wants to end the exercise, the best method to let your partner know is to tap him. Vocal signals, especially in the heat of battle, may not be heard by the other person. Two taps is the usual signal. You may also tap the mat if your opponent is too far away.

III. THE BODY POSTURE

The human body is divided into three regions: the lower extremities, the lower part of the trunk, and the upper body. The lower trunk includes the muscles supporting the spinal column. This region, in addition to connecting the upper body to the lower extremities, includes the body's largest and strongest muscles. It also includes one-third the weight of the entire body. The waist and abdominal region, therefore, can make the muscles of the whole body coordinate dynamically, and move in complete harmony. The ability to unify all parts of your body into one mass is based upon the harmonious and strong contraction of the muscles of the waist and abdominal region only.

Insofar as respiration is concerned we must mention Harumitsu Hida, a famous Japanese Zen master who trained his abdominal muscles to their highest level of perfection. He called the force exerted from the region his "correct centripetal pressure."

"In a posture that ensures correct centripetal force," wrote Hida, "you can master your will more easily, promote the unified growth of the motor nerve center, and develop the nerve fibers running to the muscles from the motor center. . . . Generally the contraction of muscles becomes better coordinated. When the sensory and motor nerve centers become sharper, there will be less chance to mistake impulses, and many kinds of exercises can be done more easily."

The body contains about five quarts of blood, but if some of it remains stationary in the abdomen—which holds about one and a half quarts—the person begins having stomachaches or constipation. If the centripetal pressure is at a high point, the blood will rush through and on to the heart. All this has to do with posture. The natural one is best for both Judo and ordinary living: feet spread apart twelve inches, torso erect while standing or sitting. Tuck the buttocks under but retain a slight arch in the lower back. This position is best for changing movements and directions easily.

IV. THE TECHNIQUES

There are many different techniques in Judo, but since the art depends mostly upon individual skill and inclination, the methods vary according to each teacher. The following outline indicates one of the most popular forms, according to Shinzo Takagaki, *kyudan* (9th Degree), a foremost authority on Judo.

1. *Tachi waza* (also known as *nage waza*): standing and throwing techniques. This is a method of throwing the opponent by way of quick and harmonious action of the body. Tachi waza includes hand throws, hip throws, feet and leg throws, and techniques of throwing the opponent by first throwing yourself on the mat, including back and side throws. Emphasis in the throwing techniques is placed on balance and minimum effort. You must first throw the opponent off-balance and place yourself in the proper position before throwing him. If you succeed in this the actual throw should take very little effort.

2. *Ne waza* (also known as *katame waza*): lying and grappling techniques. These are the holding, strangling, and armlock techniques.

3. *Atemi waza* includes methods of striking the opponent's body. Only the theory of this technique is taught today, not the practice, since Judo has become a sport.

V. THE CONTESTS

In a Judo contest only one point is needed to defeat the opponent. Because there is no second chance both contestants are under great strain. The contest itself lasts only a few seconds, although to the opponents it seems like hours. Points are awarded on the following basis:

1. A clean throw that lands the opponent on his back.

2. Holding the opponent for thirty seconds from the moment the referee calls time on the hold. If the opponent wraps his legs around yours, time is not counted. You must have complete control of his body.

3. Making the opponent give up by applying a strangle hold or by twisting an elbow joint. No part of the opponent's body may be twisted other than the elbow.

VI. PRACTICE AND TRAINING

Judo is practiced in a room called a dojo, whose floor is covered with straw matting and is usually suspended on coil springs to absorb the shock of the falls. The players wear a suit called a *judo-gi,* loose-fitting cotton trousers and a strongly woven cotton jacket. The belt should have its knot always facing front, because if it somehow slips to the side the knot could cause injury.

The training itself consists of warming up and limbering the body, free practice (*Randori*), practicing Judo principles (*Kata*), and form practice (*Uchikomi*).

Edward Snyder, a Black Belt Judo instructor at a New York YMCA, demonstrates Judo's basic techniques in the following illustrations. He is assisted by Priscilla Vasquez, one of his students.

WARM-UP EXERCISES

BODY TWIST

1. Using a natural stance, Sensei Snyder extends his arms and swings them from side to side, keeping his feet in place. This exercise should be done without straining. With practice it becomes easier to turn further.

SIDE STRETCH

2. From a relaxed stance, Sensei Snyder here leans from side to side as far as he can, again without straining. As one arm reaches toward the ground the other is brought up over the head to stretch the side muscles.

FORWARD STRETCH

3. From a standing position Sensei Snyder spreads his legs and bends forward at the waist, thrusting his arms back between his legs and curving his back. The head should be tucked in as it follows the arms through. This exercise is extremely good for the back muscles. Hesitating a moment, the follow-through is to bounce slightly into the forward position. Bending the knees is allowed.

LEAN BACK

4. This exercise is executed by raising the arms above the head and then leaning back from the waist as far as possible without straining, inhaling while leaning back, exhaling once in this position. Returning then to an upright stance, the exercise is repeated as many times as it is comfortable to do so.

NECK, SIDE TO SIDE

5. Again from a natural stance, the head is rotated slightly from side to side, lowering and raising the chin as the head moves. This exercise, in addition to relaxing the muscles in the neck, will firm up a double chin.

STRETCH FORWARD

6. From a seated position, legs straight out in front, the hands grab the ankles or as close to them as possible. The body is pulled forward as far as it will go and then bounces by pulling and releasing with the hands. This exercise is especially good for the back and leg muscles.

SIDE STRETCH

7. Seated, legs spread apart, both hands grasp one ankle and pull the body toward it. This is repeated five times and then done with the other leg.

LEG AND BACK STRETCH

8. Still seated, with legs outstretched, Sensei Snyder grasps the underside of each foot and pulls the body forward, bouncing five to ten times. This will place accent on the inside of the legs and the back.

NECK BRIDGE—On Back

9. In this exercise Sensei Snyder lies on his back, places his feet apart and balances the upper part of the body on the top of his head. This stretches the stomach muscles and strengthens the neck. After a five count the body is dropped to the floor and the whole exercise repeated.

NECK BRIDGE—On Front

10. Continuing from the previous exercise, Sensei Snyder turns over on his stomach, places his hands under his knees and pushes forward, again using his head as a balance. This stretches the back of the neck as well as the legs and the back. To do this exercise correctly, the student should inhale while rising, exhale when returning to the original position.

ART OF FALLING
(Ukemi)

REAR BREAK FALL

11. Falling properly is one of the most important phases of Judo and cannot be overestimated. It is essential not only for the execution of free and quick movements but also for the prevention of injury. *Ukemi* is the first technique to learn and master.

As illustrated here, this fall starts from a half-squat, arms extended to the front.

12. The chin is tucked in to help prevent the head from striking the mat.

13. Slapping the mat hard with the palms of the hands will aid in breaking the fall.

FRONT BREAK FALL

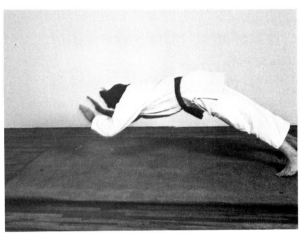

14. This fall is used when attacked from behind or pushed. From an erect stance Sensei Snyder drops forward to the ground, again slapping the mat with both hands as he hits it to break his fall. Elbows and forearms should hit the mat simultaneously. Using the hands to break the fall enables the victim to move to one side or the other and to get up quickly.

HOLDING METHODS
(kumikata)

15. Holding the opponent properly is extremely important—through your arms your opponent can anticipate your moves, and vice versa. The tightness of your hold depends on the needs of the moment, but you must control his body with your grip. Do not pull or push with the arms, but rather keep your hands in a flexed position at all times. Sensei Snyder here demonstrates how to break the hold Priscilla has on him by first gripping her sleeves on the underside.

16. By pulling down on her left sleeve and twisting her to the side, Sensei Snyder throws her off-balance and in a defensive situation would now have the advantage.

86

COLLAR GRIP

17. This time the opponent's collar is gripped with Sensei Snyder's right hand in order to break her grip. To remain in control, however, he has to throw her, since if he simply breaks her grip she can take hold of him again.

18. Pulling Priscilla forward by the neck, Sensei Snyder gets ready for the throw.

THROWING TECHNIQUES
(tachi waza)

ONE ARM SHOULDER THROW
(ippon seoi nage)

19. The principle of this technique is to place the back under the opponent's center of gravity and to throw him over the shoulder. Priscilla here looks for the right time to make her move. If the opponent is a bit stiff he can be pushed back a bit in order to be more easily drawn forward.

20. Priscilla now pulls Sensei Snyder forward, bringing his weight up on his toes.

21. Driving up hard with her shoulders and hooking his arm, Priscilla at the same time brings her right foot in front of her opponent's right foot. By stepping on the balls of her feet she easily pivots on the right foot and brings her left foot back in front of his left, turning counterclockwise as she does. Her feet are now parallel, her knees bent, and the opponent is on his toes and nestled against her back.

22. She throws him over her shoulder by springing up with her hip and pulling down hard with her arms.

23. It is important to continue to pull hard at all times in order to prevent him from dropping back into a natural position. He is now over her shoulder and heading for the mat.

24. When he hits the mat, Priscilla maintains a firm grasp on his clothing with one hand while bending his elbow with the other. This way he has no chance to retaliate.

90

LIFTING HIP THROW
(tsurikomi goshi)

25. In this case Priscilla is the opponent from whom Sensei Snyder must free himself. To do this he must bring her into a weak position by pulling her forward and lifting her up on her toes and then dropping low and throwing her over his right hip. The maneuver starts from a natural position.

26. Sensei Snyder then brings his opponent up on her toes, squats down to get leverage and begins pulling her forward.

27. Here he continues pulling the opponent over his right hip from the squatting position, maintaining his hold on the collar.

91

28. Now the opponent is parallel to the floor and falling down, head first, toward the mat. As he flips her over he pulls the collar toward him so that her head does not slam into the mat and to keep a firm grasp on her once she is down.

29. The opponent is on the mat at this point, on her back. In an actual situation the defender would continue to hold the opponent's sleeve and render him helpless.

LEG THROWS
(ashi waza)

Major Outer-Reaping Throw (o sota gari)

30. These techniques require throwing the opponent off-balance by pushing him to the rear. He will then be on only one leg and unable to retaliate.

Sensei Snyder here is the attacker, Priscilla the victim. She starts her defense by holding him in the natural position and leading him toward herself.

31. She immediately advances on him, stepping on his right side with her left foot, and attempts to throw him off-balance by pulling his right arm into her stomach with her left hand and lifting his body up and inward with her right hand. His weight has to fall on his right foot.

32. Rolling forward with her right hip, Priscilla swings her right leg behind the opponent's right leg. She strikes his right calf with her own right calf and drives her right shoulder against his chest.

33. By aiming her head toward the mat she is able to add impetus to the throw.

34. Again, the attacker's clothing should be held firmly once he's down in order to retain control of him.

MAT WORK

SIDE HOLD
(yoko shiho)

35. This is a classical hold in which the defender places one arm under the opponent's head and the other between his legs. It is necessary to keep the body low and the buttocks tucked in so that complete control over the opponent can be maintained.

NORMAL CROSS CHOKE
(nami juji jime)

36. By keeping both palms down and applying a deep collar grip, the defender's arms, which are crossed over the opponent's throat, keep him from moving out of her grasp.

95

HALF CROSS CHOKE
(kata juji jime)

37. Here one palm is up, the other is down, holding the collar taut. The palm which is down pulls and chokes the opponent.

SMOTHERING HOLD
(kami shiho gatame)

38. With the opponent on his back, the defender squats low over his head and runs her arms under his. She places her hands on his belt and pulls, pressing down on his chest as if she were a spike driving through his body.

SINGLE WING CHOKE
(kataha jime)

39. Kneeling on one leg behind the opponent, Priscilla places one arm around his neck and grabs his throat, putting the other arm behind his neck and pushing. Pushing and pulling in this manner will break the neck.

96

KARATE

I. HISTORY

Until four centuries ago Karate was not known outside China. It was limited to priests who had to defend themselves against bandits and assassins who ambushed them in mountain passages as they made their annual pilgrimages.

Traveling out of India in A.D. 525, a Buddhist monk, Bodhidharma, crossed the Chinese frontier and entered a land already exposed to Theravada and Mhayana, the two major schools of Buddhist philosophy. This self-appointed religious mission, of seemingly little consequence, is monumental when viewed in its historical perspective. In most of East Asia today, the Indian monk is revered as the spiritual father of Zen Buddhism and the founder of the weaponless fighting art called Karate.

Karate has become popular in the United States only during the last twenty years. The occupational forces in Japan during World War II brought the "Oriental dance" back with them. Before that, the Chinese migrations during the last century introduced the martial art to our West Coast, but it was practiced there almost exclusively by the Chinese.

Gogen Yamaguchi, a 5th Degree Black Belt in Karate and an international martial arts entrepreneur, has been one of the most influential promoters of Karate. He owns literally hundreds of dojos and Karate clubs in Japan.

His Karate system is Goju, which he heard about while attending school in Japan almost sixty years ago. Goju—*Go* means hard, *ju* means soft—exemplifies

Yamaguchi himself and the techniques of what is now the most popular form of Karate in the world. His teacher was Chojun Miyagi, Goju's originator, who lived in Okinawa. Miyagi received a letter from Yamaguchi inviting him to Japan so that Yamaguchi could study his system. It took little time for the businessman to realize that Goju was the best system of Karate, as it combined both the hard and soft concepts of Karate and was in keeping with the Oriental ideology that a system either too hard or too soft was only touching part of man's nature. The combination of the two, Yamaguchi knew, would make it possible for the player to use both sides of his self, Yin and Yang.

In 1939 Yamaguchi left his training and schools and went to Manchuria as an officer in the Japanese army. He was eventually captured and placed in a Russian POW camp where in a matter of days he was teaching Karate to Russian soldiers, and became the master to his captors. When he returned to Japan after the war he saw that his schools were in bad shape. The Allies, who had banned martial arts from being practiced in Japan, had somehow neglected to include Karate in their dictum. They thought it was a kind of Oriental dance, and consequently left it alone. Recently, in the United States, the art has shed much of its image as a self-defensive activity and has become more a sport.

The essential difference between self-defense and sport is that in defense one does not need to be highly trained in all the intricacies of the art, whereas in sport, since the opponents seldom attack one another or touch one another in tournaments, there must be a greater agility and knowledge of the subtle maneuvers. Technique, in other words, is the most important aspect of sport fighting.

A player trained in self-defense waits for the time he is attacked in the street or some other place where he has to defend his life. That moment seldom comes, and the self-defense player goes on with his training, limited as it is, anticipating an aggressor jumping him. The self-defense player never gets the training or achieves the ability of his counterpart, the sports player. Like all sports enthusiasts, whether he's a golfer, a ballplayer, or a skeet shooter, the Karate sports player has as his goal combat against another man in a tournament.

The amount of time one spends on training also depends upon how proficient he wishes to become. But just as the man who does too much of one thing and too little of another, the Karate player can get bogged down in routine and eventually lose interest or become stale.

II. THE PHILOSOPHY

To some, Karate has almost a religious connotation; to others it evokes images of physical violence like breaking bricks and boards with a bare hand, and combat between man and man, and man and beast. The art is basically a practice of self-defense and sport fighting which uses bare hands, arms, and wrists. In this way it is similar to Judo and sumo wrestling, except in one area. Unlike the others, Karate emphasizes use of the kick, the open-handed strike, and the closed fist strike rather than the takedown, the hold, and the throw.

In Buddhism the concept of *sunyata,* according to Alan Watts in *The Way of Zen,* is "the nature of reality, or rather, of the conceptions of reality which the human mind can form." Bruce Haines, in *Karate's History and Traditions,* furthers this notion by pointing to Nagarjuna, one of Buddhism's most revered patriarchs, who said that *sunyata* states that all things are relative and without self-nature, and that the only things that can be considered concrete or as possessing absolute properties are those that are related to other things. This is the concept of relevance, one of the most complex in Buddhism.

The scholars who relate Karate to Buddhism often rely on the word "nothingness," saying that Karate is a weaponless—and therefore empty-handed—art, and that it becomes a concrete entity only when the body is applied to the various moves and gestures that constitute the Karate defense and attack repertoire. Furthermore, when attacked by an aggressor, the Karate player responds with reflex action. Two opponents face one another in a tournament before engaging in combat. The reason for this is to clear their minds of extraneous thoughts before fighting. If they are successful in eliminating the thoughts their bodies will respond naturally from moment to moment.

Like the other martial arts, Karate is concerned with developing the mind in order to perfect the body. Bodhidharma, the founder of a school of weaponless fighting from which Karate got many of its techniques, had as his chief concern the cultivation of the mind so that one could find enlightenment. He at the same time developed a system of calisthenics designed to build mental and physical vitality to aid in the development of the power of concentration.

Today, the Karate student and teacher are engaged in a similar pursuit. The mind and body are developed simultaneously in order to perfect a unified structure, where each is working for, and not against, the other. Too often in our lives the mental process works against the body, and vice versa. In the way of Karate, if the mind tells the body not to do something, the body will not do it. What the modern-day player is concerned with is the split second decision, a decision which can only be reached when both the mental and physical parts of the body are working together.

III. WHERE TO BEGIN

There are certain exercises that you should avoid at the outset. Deep knee bends, for instance, once thought to be good for strengthening leg muscles, have in recent years been known to do more damage than it was originally thought. Deep knee bends build up leg muscles, but they also break down knee ligaments. Like weight lifters who concentrate on different parts of the body every day, alternating between the upper torso on Mondays and the lower on Tuesdays, Karate teachers work on the principle that parts of the body need a rest on alternate days for maximum benefits.

Another thing to avoid, especially at the beginning of your exercises, is going beyond your limits. Instead of building up your body, you tear it down by doing "just a few more" than your body can stand. Usually what happens in that case is the next day you can't do anything. An important thing to remember is that exercise taken in small doses with discipline can gradually be increased in intensity until, after a few short weeks, the body is in marvelous shape.

Discipline should always come from within and not be imposed from without. Working on the idea that long-term improvement is the goal, in most cases you will be able to achieve greater results and be healthier in a shorter period of time. The discipline should be focused on the exercises themselves by concentrating only on the part of the body being developed. If you find yourself thinking about how many exercises you still have to do before quitting for the day, take a deep breath, sending all your energy to the part being worked on. All negative, extraneous thoughts will disappear. Furthermore, it's never a good idea to count. Do what you think you're capable of. There's a school of thought that states that one should do more repetitions each day. What those who advocate this do not realize is that the person's body changes each day, along with his inclinations. If you feel ten repetitions are enough, do ten. If the next day, twenty fit you better, do that many.

Certain of the martial arts stress standing in one place for long periods of time. Some experts pass this off as meaningless and "counterproductive." What they don't seem to realize is that a stationary position is intended not solely to tone up the body but also to stabilize the mind. By holding a position for a long period of time, the mind has a chance to send energy into the body, getting it ready for the physical exercise. One must be *willing* to exert energy before the exercise means anything.

IV. WHAT TO DO AND HOW TO DO IT

Deep breathing, which is an essential component in all the martial arts, must be practiced with regularity. It requires nothing special, no specific time nor space. Sitting at a table, standing up, walking along, anywhere one feels the spurt of energy, deep breathing can be the most beneficial of all the exercises.

One important thing to remember is that in whatever you do, your breathing should be maintained at a normal rate. When exercising, people tend to think that short bursts of breath are necessary. Not true. In Karate every motion and exercise is a natural one. Avoid sharp intake of breath; instead, concentrate on breathing normally as you proceed. It will also take any edge off the exercises themselves —how many you have to do and what kind. By sending the air into your lower abdomen you smooth out jerky motions, making the entire process a natural flow.

The most frequent cause of poor breathing is bad posture. Slumping over or slouching reduces lung capacity. People slump for various reasons, none of them justifiable—laziness, habit, fatigue, weak muscles, or self-consciousness due to excessive weight or height. To breathe properly, however, correct posture is a must.

An expanded chest, to the ordinary person, indicates a pompous nature. But look at athletes. Their expanded chests are the result of proper breathing, of driving the air into their diaphragms, and not, as most people do, into their stomachs. Along with the breathing, endurance exercises are high on the list of priorities insofar as initial exercises are concerned. Jumping rope, riding a bicycle, running, swimming increase your stamina once you get to the other steps. Weight lifting is good for improving the strength of your arms. Also helpful, when modified, are the knee bends mentioned earlier. Avoid deep knee bends, and instead do half-squats, bending slightly at the knees as if you were playing shortstop, waiting for the batter to knock a ground ball in your direction.

Another misconception about exercises has to do with sit-ups. Previously, the straight-legged approach was considered the best, but now, after doctors have said straight legs cause too much stress and strain, the bent leg method is the best, relieving strain in the lower back. Before going into the techniques it is important to know some exercises you might try.

The starting position, which should be assumed before every exercise, finds your feet spread apart at shoulder width. Your arms should dangle by your sides. If there is any tenseness in your arms or in the rest of your body, shake it out. Breathe at a normal pace, but lengthen the inhalation and exhalation, sending the air to the spot three inches below your navel.

V. SOME WARM-UPS

In these warm-up exercises the count numbers are mentioned because beginners have a tendency to do as many as they can before falling down from exhaustion. They are not meant as rigid restrictions but should give a general idea of how long to pursue each exercise. The aim is to complete all the exercises rather than to concentrate on one or two, thus giving equal attention to all parts of the body. As you practice these exercises your body will become better toned and it will be easier to do more repetitions of each exercise. When this facility is acquired, the count system should be dropped and the state of your body will dictate how long to practice each exercise.

One: Warm-up

By rotating your neck from side to side for ten counts or so you'll be able to eliminate what you've seen older people do—when they turn to see something their entire body turns with the neck. This is caused by stiffness. It's one thing to have unity in motion, it's quite another when you do it because you're unable to turn one part of the body at a time.

To deemphasize a double chin open your mouth wide and drop your chin toward your chest. Then, close your mouth and lean your head back, trying to visualize the crown touching the small of your back. Do not overexert yourself on this one at first. With practice, the muscles will loosen and the chin become firmer. For those who want to combine the two, rotate your head in a circle, opening your mouth at six o'clock and close it up at twelve.

Two: Warm-up

From the starting position, breathe in deeply while raising your arms, and then exhale while dropping the arms as close to the floor as you can without bending over. Ten counts are suggested at first.

Three: Warm-up

With your hands on your hips, knees slightly bent, rotate your body in a circle, bending forward, to the side, and back as far as you can without straining. The waist, abdomen, and lower back muscles will benefit most from this exercise. Five counts clockwise, five counterclockwise to begin with.

Four: Warm-up

Stand perfectly straight, knees slightly bent, arms out in a straight line from the shoulders. Bend to the right as far as you can, lifting your left arm over your head. Five counts are suggested. Repeat the process on your left side. You'll be able to feel the muscles on either side pulling. Do not press right away.

Since the part of the body that goes first is the waist, these exercises will tone up the muscles and, hopefully, with enough practice, solidify the abdominal and lower back muscles.

Five: Touching Toes

Another exercise for both the waist and legs is Touching Toes. From a natural stance with knees slightly bent, reach down with your right hand and touch your left foot. Return to an upright position. Alternate the exercise by touching your right foot for twenty counts.

Six: Isometrics

One essential thing to remember is that natural breathing is a must in doing all exercises. While individuals will more often than not remember to breathe regularly while doing stretching exercises, they seem to forget while doing isometrics. The tension feels greater in isometrics, and many hold their breath while performing them.

One of the most popular of the isometric exercises utilizes the arms. By clasping your hands in front of you try to pull them apart. Breathe in first before starting. While you apply pressure, breathe out. Repeat this five times.

Reverse the process, placing a balled fist into the palm of your other hand and push. Concentrate not on skin against skin but trying to push your balled fist through the other hand, trying to penetrate the skin on the outside of it.

Another exercise has an up-and-down motion. Ball the fist of your right hand. Place it, palm upward, before you. With your other hand grab the wrist of the right hand and push down, while at the same time trying to raise your right hand up. Reverse the process for a ten count.

Another one for the arms and hands: Stand in a doorway and press your hands against the wood on either side. Remember to take a deep breath before beginning and exhale slowly while applying the pressure.

Neck isometrics: Place your hands on your forehead and press backward while trying to push your head forward through the hands. Next, place your hands behind your neck and press forward while pushing your head backward toward your hands. Repeat five times.

Demonstrating techniques employed in Karate in the following illustrations is Jerry Gardner, 3rd Degree Black Belt and one of the most diversified of the martial artists, having studied Judo, Aikido, Jujitsu, and Kung Fu, as well as Karate. He is joined by his teacher, Chaka Zulu.

STRETCHING
EXERCISES

1. By placing both hands flat on the ground just below the right knee, Jerry straightens his right leg, heel on the floor. His left leg, slightly bent at the knee, is off to the left. His head is almost touching his right kneecap. Bouncing the head on the knee is good for the back and shoulder muscles. Also, by pushing up on the hands, bouncing is again possible, this time stretching the upper leg muscles.

2. This exercise is also for the legs and arms. With the left foot placed squarely on the ground and the right leg extended toward the rear, Jerry bounces slightly on the left leg, bending at the knee. The back is kept straight. The arm muscles are tightened and loosened one after the other. In doing this, it helps to imagine pushing against walls on either side.

3. Illustrated here is another leg stretch, similar to the one in Figure 1, except that the left leg is more to the front, and the hands, rather than being on either side of the left leg, are now in front of the body, slightly off the floor. It is important to bounce more in this one, stretching both the upper and lower leg muscles and those in the back. At all times, wherever the hands may be placed, by imagining pushing down on a hard surface the arms, too, will benefit from the stretching. The sensation is similar to that found in isometrics.

4. This exercise starts from an upright stance, hands at the sides. Then, with his arms above his head, palms out and no more than six inches from one another, Jerry slowly leans the upper half of his body back as far as he can and still maintain his balance. His palms are facing in the same direction, as if he were pushing against a wall. This exercise is good for the abdominal muscles as well as the back.

STEP AND PUNCH

5. Jerry assumes a Zen wide stance, with the feet spread apart, the left in front of the right, which is cocked behind. The left hand is down and in front in a low block position. The right hand is in its chamber, fist up, tucked in at the side. He is getting ready for a crescent step, a semicircular movement executed with his right foot.

6. He now steps into position by bringing the right foot to the left, his hands remaining stationary.

7. Jerry then executes the punch by bringing out his right hand and pulling his left hand into chamber at the side. The right foot has moved out in front along with the right hand, completing the crescent step. In this technique, as in most Karate movements, when the left hand is forward and the right is in chamber, or vice versa, the movement itself shifts rapidly with an in-and-out thrust.

FIGHTING STANCE

8. This is actually a variation on a Kung Fu stance, with the left hand high and forward, while the right hand is placed near the forearm of the left. The left foot is placed in the direction of the blow.

KICKING TECHNIQUES

CHAMBER FOR SIDE KICK

9. By balancing on one foot, Jerry lifts the other foot as high as he can—the higher the lift or chamber, the higher the kick. The Karate player always looks in the direction of his attack. In this case to the left. The fists are knotted and pulled back toward the body, and the toes of the left foot are pointed up. The kick will be delivered with the ball of the foot. The image here is that of cocking a trigger before pulling it.

SIDE KICK

10. In this particular kick the opponent will be hit with the heel of the foot. The left leg has shot out like a bullet at the opponent, and the left arm follows it. The right arm is kept in the chamber by the right side, ready to strike after the initial kick.

FRONT SNAP KICK

11. Here Jerry pushes down hard with his arms, as if driving them through the floor, to give more momentum to the kick. Rising from the floor, Jerry's foot is powered not to the solar plexus but through it to the other side of the opponent's body. This lends more force to the kick, as does the flat foot which has more impact than either the ball or heel alone.

CHAMBER FOR THE ROUNDHOUSE KICK

12. With the right foot implanted on the ground, the left foot is raised high, knee bent back in order to get as much thrust as possible. The body shifts slightly right in order to gather power for the kick.

13. The execution of the kick itself shows the foot being thrust forward. The toes are up, pulled back toward the leg. It's as if the toes were tied by a string to the knee. The kick is done with the ball of the foot. The hands move higher on the body, the left palm in front of the face and facing it. The right hand, also with the palm open, faces the opponent.

14. After the roundhouse kick is completed the player returns to a fighting stance. This one is the reverse of the stance pictured in Figure 8. The right leg has been brought back, and the hands have exchanged positions.

110

BACK KICK

15. Here Jerry moves into position for the back kick. His head is turned in the direction of the kick, his feet are together, and his left hand is extended beyond the right hand.

16. The execution of the kick shows the left leg vaulted high. His hands are thrust in front of him to give him balance, which he maintains by keeping his weight evenly distributed on the right foot. His head is still turned to the left, giving him two advantages: He can see what damage he's done, and, by keeping his head up, there is less chance of losing his balance.

17. After he has executed the kick Jerry swings his body around and assumes the fighting stance again.

FLYING FRONT KICK

18. Jerry first assumes the fighting stance. During the technique he will come far into the foreground—in the flying kicks the Karate player never returns to the original position because in these kicks he is always on the attack.

19. In the execution of the technique, he pushes off the ground with the right leg. The left leg, the one that will kick, is high and bent at the knee. The right hand is in chamber.

112

20. As the body returns to the ground, on the right foot, the left foot is thrust forward in the kick, with the left hand following it.

21. Here Jerry returns to the fighting stance. Notice how far from the wall he has come in the execution of the kick. He is at least three feet farther forward than at the outset.

Y-PONS—Front Kick and Takedown Technique

22. Jerry and Chaka Zulu assume the positions of a Y-Pon, a practice form of Karate which is not meant for sparring purposes. Rather, it is the ideal form of the martial art. They are prepared for a crescent step and punch, with Jerry as the attacker. His right arm is in chamber by his right side; his left arm is pointed down, balled in a fist.

23. As Jerry steps forward and punches with his right arm, Chaka blocks the stroke away softly with his own right. Instead of trying to abruptly halt it, Chaka flows with the movement of the punch. His left arm is still at his side, palm up and open. He is not yet ready to retaliate, but still on the defensive.

24. Chaka now grabs Jerry's *gi* (uniform) at the elbow, and with a front kick drives his right leg into his midsection. In Karate so many kicks and punches are thrown to the solar plexus because it is where the Chi energy is stored. By attacking that part of the body, the opponent is rendered helpless for a moment, just enough time here to throw Jerry off-balance. Chaka's left fist is balled as he readies to attack with it.

25. Chaka throws a high punch to Jerry's chin with his left arm, maintaining his hold on Jerry's gi at the right elbow. In the previous picture, Jerry was already being spun around, away from Chaka, by the force of Chaka's kick. As soon as Chaka sends his left arm toward Jerry's face, he brings his foot to the floor for balance.

26. With his hand still on Jerry's right arm, Chaka kicks up with his left foot, catching Jerry under the right knee, tripping him, and throwing him off-balance. Jerry is swept to the ground.

27. Chaka has not yet let go of Jerry's right arm and here holds it over his left knee. In this position he could easily break Jerry's elbow.

Y-PONS—Horse Stance

28. Chaka here is presenting the fists, the ready position. His feet are together, toes pointed out at a 45-degree angle, while his hands hang by his sides.

29. Next he steps into a horse stance. His right hand is at first in its chamber. As he steps out to the left he extends his right arm, as if to grab his opponent's gi.

30. This is another example of the arm and hand action in Karáte—when the right hand is in chamber the left hand is extended. The movement is fast as the hands change position, somewhat like a piston.

FIGHTING STANCE
FOR SPARRING

31. Jerry and Chaka are ready-
ing themselves for sparring.
Each has his left foot forward,
left arm extended, and right
arm cocked in its chamber.

32. Jerry moves his right foot
forward of his left and begins
to attack by bringing his right
arm around.

118

33. He then attempts a round-house kick, which Chaka blocks with his left hand. Chaka's right hand is prepared to strike.

34. With his left hand still on Jerry's left leg Chaka sweeps his right arm under his opponent's legs and strikes his groin. But rather than just punching, Chaka grabs Jerry here and pulls him to the floor, leaving him writhing in pain.

Y-PON—Spinning Technique

35. Chaka stands in the starting position. Jerry has his right arm in chamber, left arm down and forward. He is in a low block position, ready to step in and punch.

36. As Jerry throws the punch, Chaka steps easily to the side, spinning away from his opponent.

37. Chaka continues to spin until he finds himself at Jerry's rear. He jumps on his opponent's back and strikes with both hands to his collarbone, simultaneously striking his kidneys with his feet.

38. After Jerry is dropped to the floor, Chaka punches him with his right hand in the face. Throughout the technique, Chaka has held onto Jerry's uniform.

KUNG FU

I. HISTORY

Kung Fu (or Gung Fu), supposedly the most violent of the martial arts, dates back many centuries. Its history is filled with facts and figures, myths and legends. Originally a Chinese art developed to utilize the components of the human body and traditional Chinese weapons, Kung Fu trained young men who spent years in temples studying the techniques.

Kung Fu's proper term, *wu-shu* or *gwa-shu,* meaning martial art or national art, originally came about when priests crossed over mountain ranges between China and India. The priests were attacked by bandits and had to use whatever means they had to protect themselves against the attackers. They carried their supplies in four heavy baskets that were balanced on a staff or long stick riding on their shoulders. When the bandits attacked, the priests simply let the baskets slip from the staffs and would use the staffs as weapons.

Since most of Kung Fu's movements were—and are—based on animal techniques, the students sought to perfect their ability by copying even more diligently the actions of certain creatures. From the tiger, for instance, the student learned to move with greater speed, strength, and agility. He also emulated its clawing and pawing and the rapid snap of the tiger's arm. From the crane he learned grace and hooking or grabbing moves, actions stemming from out-stretched hands, fingers curled slightly, and the lightning-fast strike or hook. From the monkey he learned to feint, to deceive his opponent by throwing himself into what would appear to be an off-balance posture, attempting to make his enemy overconfident.

Fighting was not the only thing taught in the temples. The philosophy behind it was equally important. Like T'ai Chi Ch'uan, called Kung Fu's shadowboxing because of its less ferocious techniques, Kung Fu depends upon Chi energy, the universal life force within each person. Mental determination and power must be developed before the physical prowess can be activated. The two must meet in unison for perfection.

II. THE STYLES

Two distinct styles emerged from the temple training, the hard and the soft, into which the numerous variations can be divided. The essential difference between these two basic styles is in the direction and patterns of their respective forms, and in the emphasis of their training methods.

Cho-li-fat, the hard style, emphasizes power and strength, offensive maneuvers designed for quick and debilitating attacks on the opponent. With its preference for stabbing and clawing and circling hand motions, some of which are reminiscent of "haymakers" or roundhouse punches, the hard style Kung Fu player is out to devastate the opposition. The major weakness of this style is the absence of foot maneuvers, although in some schools kicking techniques are taught.

Sil-lum, the soft style, translated as "young forest," means that the practitioner should be supple and flexible—able to bend like a young tree in the wind. This style depends on speed and agility, the quick thrust, hand maneuvers that attack vulnerable parts of the body. While the hard style player uses force to go after any part of the opponent's body, overpowering him with strength, the soft stylist attacks only certain parts of the body that are more susceptible than others.

The soft style is much more popular today as it keeps more in touch with the philosophy behind the martial art. Brute strength is not the key to Kung Fu perfection, but rather humility, wisdom, and perseverance. One must know when to take life and when to spare it. Learning to meditate, to concentrate on the universe within us, and to achieve a quietness of the soul are the goals. When philosophers talk of simplicity they are not referring to a lack of complexity. Instead they are catering to the notion that wisdom is a gentle process of understanding the spirit behind the action.

The late Bruce Lee was once asked to elaborate on one of the essentials of his *Jeet June Do* method of Kung Fu. "The best illustration is something I borrowed from Ch'an [Zen]," Lee began. "Before I studied the art, a punch to me was just like a punch, a kick just like a kick. After I learned the art, a punch is no longer a punch, a kick no longer a kick. Now that I've understood the art, a punch is just like a punch, a kick just like a kick. The height of cultivation is really nothing special. It is merely simplicity, the ability to express the utmost with the minimum. . . . It is basically sophisticated fighting style stripped to its essentials.''

Lee's style was a combination of Western fencing and the *Wing Chun* style, simple, direct, and nonclassical. The Wing Chun system, one of the most popular in the modern age, appeared in China over three hundred and fifty years ago in the Fatshun County of the Canton Province. Unlike the exclusively hard style which dotes on attack, Wing Chun combines both the hard and the soft, but stays primarily with the defensive characteristics of the art.

Wing Chun was invented by a woman, Yim Wing Chun, who learned part of the system from a Buddhist nun. Because Yim Wing Chun realized that women were not as strong as men she brought in techniques which used the center of the body as the attack and defense zones. All the punches in Wing Chun move at their opponent in a straight line—never from the shoulder—in order to conserve energy. A punch, for instance, never strikes from outside the boundaries of the shoulder. The player also uses low kicks, instead of the exquisite high kicks used in the harder systems, because in the high shots there is a greater chance of losing one's balance. The Wing Chun method is popular since it combines both the soft and the hard, borrowing the best from each.

III. GENERAL THEORY

Directness and simplicity are the mainstays of Kung Fu: The elaborate classical moves are mostly for show and not, as most people think, for films and matches. The soft-style player, rather than overpowering the opponent with strength, often goes after the eyes and groin, the areas most vulnerable to attack. Unlike other systems that use circular movements, Kung Fu economically states that a straight punch is both the most powerful way to strike and the most difficult to defend against.

The physical activity of Kung Fu is not bound to the superstitions and archaic social attitudes surrounding it. As a test of physical endurance and healthy approach to living, the art is at its most valuable position.

The ''secretness'' surrounding Kung Fu has prevented the public from learning of its ability to physically benefit the practitioner (an unwritten law prohibited masters from teaching the art to non-Chinese until 1964 when Wong Ark-Yuey opened his doors to all races in Los Angeles). Physical education teachers, for instance, who have been asked to include Kung Fu training in their classes, refused because of the bad publicity on the art. They had been told that Kung Fu's prime goal was to kill the adversary, sometimes by simply poking him with a finger. Films depicting the violence associated with Kung Fu have not helped its image, but at least the public is getting something in these blood and guts extravaganzas that allows them to peek into what before was a total mystery.

Our attitudes toward the martial arts in general had also to do with cultural significance. Bowing before the temple before a match had always been thought of as a prerequisite to performing the arts. And, unfortunately, most people were under the impression that Oriental accouterments, like temples and special uniforms, were necessary if one were to excel in these mysterious activities.

"Kung Fu," the television show, alleviated much of that since David Carradine as Caine practices his art without the folderol of his ancestors. The television show has also made it clear that Kung Fu is not a completely aggressive fighting art. In fact, as Caine illustrates, he is almost always on the defensive, being attacked first before he acts.

It is not necessary to accept Kung Fu only as a method of self-defense but also as a means by which we can become healthy and physically fit individuals. Kung Fu is by no means the most accessible nor the best form of exercise, nor is it superior to the other martial arts, but it is certainly useful on its own terms.

In addition to its fitness benefits, the art is also important as a recreational endeavor. Practicing Kung Fu can actually be enjoyable. Whereas some form of exercise can be tedious for their lack of variation, Kung Fu is very intricate in its forms and techniques. Furthermore, whether a person is involved in the Wing Chun method or one of the other numerous forms, he does have a choice. The personal preference aspect is an attractive one, for each person has the opportunity to choose his own style.

An additional feature is that people of all ages can participate, and at their own rate. The older one gets does not necessarily mean he gets better, but he does get wiser, and when we see ninety-nine-year-old champions practicing in a classroom, we come to understand that the martial arts, more than most forms of exercise, can be undertaken until the day we die.

IV. KUNG FU AND HEALTH

Good health, whether approached from a martial arts standpoint or sought through instructions from the American Medical Association, is really based on simple common sense. Exercise, nourishing foods, correct posture and breathing, proper rest, and a positive mental attitude are generally accepted means of insuring physical well-being. Kung Fu practitioners have the added benefit of a system that seeks to strengthen and build not only the body but the mind and spirit as well—and with equal concentration.

As the student progresses in his study of Kung Fu he will discover he is enjoying better health and a sounder physique. The following shows specifically how the various parts of the body are affected by the faithful practice of this art.

1. A well-balanced nervous system is one of the most valuable benefits of practicing Kung Fu since the nervous system affects all other bodily functions. A Kung Fu player pauses before going into combat to relax his nervous system by removing all extraneous thoughts from his mind, thus giving him greater concentration and control. Through the exercises given at the end of this section and development of the power of meditation, the Kung Fu student will be able to govern his nervous system and its responses, leading to better all-round health as well as improved combatant ability.

2. Most Kung Fu masters say that proper breathing is the most important exercise in the entire martial arts system. Deep breathing means that the air is taken in and sent to the psychic center of the body, three inches below the navel. In modern terms, to breathe down to that area is the method of diaphragmatic breathing controlled by the mind. The exercise is invaluable because the contraction and expansion of the diaphragm and abdominal muscles constantly alter the abdominal pressure. Furthermore, the movement of the diaphragm produces massaging effects on the liver and strengthens its function. And finally, a long period of continual breathing exercise helps stave off fatigue.

3. The exercises taught in Kung Fu have a positive effect on the digestive system. Since the waist and abdomen are the mainsprings in the practice of this art, the exercises aid in the secretion of juices from the stomach, liver, intestines, and pancreas.

4. The exercises benefit the reproductive organs. The old school of thought states that abstinence from sexual intercourse is an absolute necessity. What the old school fails to understand is that at puberty spermatogenesis in the male and ovulation in the female begin. Sexual intercourse, therefore, should be treated naturally since it is a normal human activity. Refraining from sex has no beneficial effects.

One of the most important aspects in maintaining a healthy body is posture. When doing the exercises the Kung Fu practitioner should examine his form and posture from the head to the neck, shoulders, elbows, wrists, fingers, chest, waist, the space between the legs and knees, to determine if they are in a natural posture. The first illustration at the end of this section is an example of natural posture.

The next thing to check for is natural breathing, making sure it complies with a natural expansion and contraction of the lungs. The object is to utilize mind over force, mental control over unnecessary strain. The following information on form and posture will enable the student to complete the exercises with greater ease.

1. The Head. Imagine that your head is suspended by a string attached to the crown. As a result the chin will angle downward toward the chest. The reason for this is protection of the neck, a vulnerable spot for an opponent to attack. The suspended head also allows one to be more alert, and furthermore puts the head, spine, and coccyx in a straight line.

2. The Shoulders. When the shoulders are drooping and in a relaxed state the Kung Fu practitioner is better able to complete the exercises and throw a punch in combat than if the shoulders are raised and tense. Drooping your shoulders does not mean that you fall forward, but rather that you are in a relaxed position. The body is still erect. In order to loosen up your shoulders shake your arms by your side, letting the shoulders relax.

3. The Chest. By loosening the chest you will aid abdominal breathing and move your center of gravity lower so that the breathing will be deep and long. Loosening the chest does not mean it will contract; on the contrary, it will remain relaxed while you still maintain a straight and centered but not stiff posture. Tensing the chest, by strenuously contracting and expanding it, causes abnormally rapid breathing and a raising of the center of gravity, both of which would impede the correct position of the internal organs.

4. The Back. There are two spinal curves from the head to the buttocks: One is at the junction between the neck and the thoracic vertebrae and the other is between the lumbar vertebrae and the buttocks. The aim of the exercises taught in Kung Fu is to align the head, spine, and coccyx (the beaklike bone at the end of the spine, located between the cleft of the buttocks). What all this means is that by straightening the spinal column the circulation and nutrition of the spinal cord will be enhanced and the body will be kept in better balance.

5. The Waist. The waist is the link between the upper and lower parts of the body. While it is a good idea to have a firm waist, it is also essential to keep it relaxed at all times during the exercises.

When moving through the techniques and exercises in Kung Fu and the other martial arts it is necessary to move the entire body at once. That is, do not attempt an attack with only your arms or your feet. The power and force behind the movements come from the entire body generating its energy in the direction of the target. Since the waist is the link between the upper and lower torso, tenseness in the waist muscles will cause tenseness in all the body muscles. Use your mental powers to consciously relax the waist muscles.

6. The Buttocks. By loosening the above mentioned parts of the body, the buttocks would naturally become loosened as well. In the exercises and in daily walking, the buttocks should be tucked in. Practice by pushing forward with your hips. Use no strain, however, since it would tighten the muscles and throw off your body balance.

7. The Legs. Many times when a martial arts player executes his movements in a clumsy manner, the fault lies in incorrect postures and forms of the waist and legs. The movements of the legs combine those of the knees, feet, toes, the footwork of advancing, retreating, sidestepping, standing in equilibrium, and the acceleration of movement. Since maneuverability comes mostly from the lower body, the legs themselves must be both developed and coordinated in a way that expedites that maneuverability. When exercising the legs it becomes necessary to use both legs simultaneously. In this way you will be able to maintain coordination.

V. MEMORIZING THE ROUTINES

Spending a few minutes each day concentrating on the routines will not only aid in remembering them but will also assist you in other activities. When you try to memorize the techniques place all your mental concentration on learning them. When you finally do comprehend them, you will be able to execute them more proficiently, especially in terms of blocking out all extraneous thoughts.

During the memorization process make sure you tackle the movements in sequence, starting with the basic exercises and moving on to the techniques themselves. In that way you will form a thought pattern, at once linear and infinitely more comprehensible.

The advantages of this learning process cannot be emphasized too much. The fact that one technique flows naturally into the other will enhance your ability to organize the sequence and place each technique in its proper perspective. For example, before you practice each technique, you should first create a mental picture of it, watching yourself going through the movements, maintaining balance, shifting your weight from one side to the other, striking, retreating.

Also, before you actually begin the exercises you should establish the correct breathing pattern, relax your muscles, concentrate only on the technique itself, and establish the sequence of events. By the time you're ready for the technique itself you will have already locked it in your mind. Think of it as a pregame show, a psychic warm-up. You will be pleasantly surprised how easily it will go.

There are two separate ways of memorizing the material. Choose the one that suits you best.

The Short-Group Method

This is the most advantageous method for one who has a limited practice time and who is also doing it by himself. The Short-Group is a step-by-step process by which you will take one small portion of the technique at a time. Memorize it thoroughly and then go on to the next until you have learned it completely. The reason for this is that since you have no one to assist you, you will have to refer to the book every so often. We tend to forget key movements if we try to learn too much at one time.

The Short Group is also valuable in between classes if you are attending school. When you return to the classroom (*kwoon*) you will be that much more accomplished.

The Long-Group Method

This is the method in which two or more people are practicing simultaneously. Your partner can read the sections to you, and you can read them to him. The flow will not be as broken in this method as it is in the Short-Group.

Your retention level will be greater in the Long-Group because the sequence is not interrupted. The movements are read to you more rapidly by your partner, and his ability to correct you on the spot will eliminate the time it takes for you to pick up the manual. If no partner is available, seek out someone who is content to read the sequences to you without going through the movement himself.

When you look at the pictures and the accompanying explanations, study them carefully. Do not simply watch the movements, but also look for weight distribution, the angles from which the arms and legs come, where one movement terminates and the next begins. Check head position, posture, and remember to loosen your muscles. Admittedly, this is a lot to contend with, especially for the beginner, but in order to do them correctly you must practice continually.

Practice time will be according to your own time schedule, but it is a good idea to practice at certain times of the day. Just as you will have to learn the sequences in a pattern, you should also choose a particular time of the day to go through the techniques.

The best time is in the morning just after getting out of bed. The rest of the day will be filled with positive Chi energy. Think of it this way: You will go into the day with deep, steady breathing, coordination, mental concentration, an erect posture, and a healthy attitude.

In the following illustrations Chung K. Chow demonstrates the movements basic to his Wing Chun system of Kung Fu. Mr. Chow is a Hong Kong native who came to this country in 1971. He currently owns and operates the New York Wing Chun Kung Fu Academy. His partner here is Jerry Gardner, the Karate Black Belt pictured in the illustrations in the previous chapter. As one of Mr. Chow's students, Jerry has become a Kung Fu master.

TRADITIONAL STANCE

1. Mr. Chow illustrates this stance, his right arm extended in front of him with a balled fist. He will strike with this hand, while his left, with an open palm designed to both defend against retaliation and to slash at the opponent if there is an opening, is brought in front of his chest. The feet are apart, with most of the weight on the rear foot.

2. This is the same traditional stance viewed from the front. Chow is well protected against attack. With his feet in this stance he is able to move either to the side, or back, or to the front.

130

THE CRANE

3. Chow's imitation of a crane here suggests the soft style of Kung Fu in which the blows are knifelike, quick and deadly. The back of his hands are calloused from slicing them against wooden ''horses'' and hard punching bags. The left hand, raised to shoulder level, protects the upper body, while the right, palm open and facing to the right, is in a defensive gesture.

THE SNAKE

4. Kung Fu is combat at close range, particularly in the snake form which takes place in a very small area. The palms are again open. The right is aimed at the neck of the opponent while the left is pointed at his midsection. Chow looks like a cobra ready to strike, body back and coiled, set to spring at the adversary.

WING OF BIRD

5. In Kung Fu two-man forms and series include the attack, the defense, and the counterattack. Sparring techniques in Kung Fu are generally very stylized. The players do not often enter tournament competition because they would rather practice in private. The nature of Kung Fu still dictates that the art be reserved to classrooms and not be on display as public spectacles.

Here Jerry and Chow assume the traditional starting position, except that the feet and arm positions are opposite. Jerry is in a standard attack stance, something like boxing, left hand in front and parrying, right hand back waiting for the power punch.

6. Jerry has initiated this movement, throwing his left at Chow's face. Chow has blocked it with his right shoulder, while bringing his left hand up in order to grab Jerry's wrist.

132

7. Chow has grabbed the wrist and pulls Jerry down and toward him. His right fist is balled, ready to strike Jerry's face.

8. By continuing to pull Jerry down, Chow punches his face. In order to ward off the blow, Jerry brings his right arm high, pushing the punch away. Neither man has moved his feet during this contest. The technique calls for close combat with use of the upper body and arms only. Any movement in the legs would be for balance alone.

PUNCH BLOCK

9. This technique finds the players in the middle of sparring. Jerry has thrown a punch to Chow's chest, and Chow has moved back slightly, placing most of his weight on his rear foot. He is ready to ward off the blow by leaning to his left and pushing the hand away to his right.

10. Chow, using a circular movement, moves further to his left and brings his right hand up. Jerry, anticipating a counterattack, also brings up his hand. Notice that a weight shift has occurred. In the previous picture, Jerry was the aggressor, moving in toward Chow. Now, he is pulling back. Kung Fu, more than the other martial arts, uses a give-and-take situation in sparring.

11. Chow assumes the snake form as he brings his right arm toward Jerry's eyes. He is uncoiling and springing toward his opponent, lightning-quick.

12. Jerry has not had time to block the cobra sting as Chow slices through the air on his way to the eyes. Again, the feet have not moved.

135

DOUBLE STICKY HANDS
(With No Movement)

13. Sticky hands gets its name from the way the opponents jockey their hands and arms for position. The hands literally tumble over one another until the right time comes to strike. This is the exercise students practice most often in Kung Fu training areas. The object behind it is being able to anticipate the opponent's actions. Many accomplished players do it blindfolded, and the results are amazing. Just when it seems the opponent will land a blow, the blindfolded player will throw an arm in the air and block it. In Kung Fu it is essential to comprehend the space around you, the actions and reactions of the opponent and how to contend with them.

The feet are stationary in this sticky-hand technique. Jerry has his eyes closed—by being blind to his opponent's motions he can transfer his sight into the feelings and sensations he gets as his arms and hands tumble over Chow's.

14. From the side Sticky Hands looks like a wave rolling gently toward the shore. As one arm rises the other drops.

136

DOUBLE STICKY HANDS—
(With Movement)

15. The main difference between this and the Double Sticky Hands with No Movement is that the legs move as each player slips into an advantageous position.

This time both players' eyes are open and the bodies are more mobile. Their facial expressions reveal their awareness, anticipating each other's moves. In this picture both men are on equal footing.

16. Here Jerry has become the aggressor. His arms are extended and his weight moves forward. Chow, on the other hand, sets up in a defensive stance. Chow's eyes are fixed on Jerry's neck, the spot where he can best see Jerry's entire bodily movement.

17. Chow is now on the counteroffensive. He moves slightly to his left, also leaning back a bit, and is ready to attack.

18. In a lightning-quick move, Chow snaps his right foot forward toward Jerry, causing Jerry to back off, pulling his left foot back and away from Chow.

19. Chow throws Jerry off-balance and causes him to take his eyes off his total motion. Jerry's body is now turned toward where Chow's hands are moving. Chow has released his left hand from Jerry's arm and has shifted it over to grab Jerry's left wrist. Chow's right hand comes up ready to strike Jerry's face.

20. By grabbing Jerry's left wrist, Chow is able to keep his opponent's left side under control while at the same time preventing his right arm from coming up for a blow.

KICKING TECHNIQUES

PUNCH-KICK

21. The basic kicking techniques are different from those in the other martial arts because of the classic style. In Kung Fu they are executed more as a performance than as a method of devastation. Illustrated here is a combination punch-kick technique. Jerry will throw a punch at Chow who in turn will move to his left in an attempt to block it.

22. Chow continues to move to his left, shoving the punch aside and bringing his foot up toward Jerry's knee. The joints are areas quite vulnerable to attack.

23. Chow's foot drives into Jerry's knee, while at the same time Chow throws a punch at his face. Chow's right hand has also grabbed Jerry's, which turns Jerry to the side. Jerry is completely helpless now. He can neither retaliate nor block Chow's thrusts.

KICK WITH HEEL

24. Here Jerry throws a punch that Chow blocks with his right hand. Instead of blocking it by pushing it off to Jerry's right, Chow attempts to edge it to Jerry's left.

25. Chow's blocking arm grabs hold of Jerry's right wrist, bringing it down toward the floor. At the same time, Chow brings his right leg up and kicks it into Jerry's midsection. In this, as in other kicking techniques, the player tries turning his opponent away from him to reduce the chances for a counterattack.

26. Chow did not push his opponent far enough, for Jerry counters here with a punch thrown at Chow's face. But Chow is ready. He blocks the punch with his right hand.

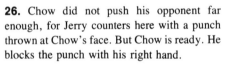

142

SINGLE STICKY HAND

27. In this technique, one arm is placed behind the back, using the stronger one. Their toes are touching as Jerry wraps his left arm over Chow's right.

28. Chow drops his arm underneath his opponent's and brings his weight slightly forward as he tries to throw a punch at Jerry. Chow never takes his eyes off Jerry's neck. Jerry, incorrectly, watches the hand action more than he does his opponent. He, too, should be concentrating on his opponent's neck area in order to know best what will happen next.

29. Chow throws the punch, but it is blocked by Jerry turning his arm inward to ward it off. Jerry's next move would be to throw his wrist in Chow's face, but Chow is in a position to block by bringing his arm down. It is just as important to leave yourself protected after a missed punch as it is to throw it.

THE POWER PUNCH

30. Here Jerry is in a wide fighting stance and punching.

31. The pumping action in Kung Fu acts somewhat like a car piston. One fist after another rams forward and then back into chamber under the shoulder. In addition to achieving balance and coordination, the player doing these movements can also shift his weight back and forth.

ANTIMUGGING DEFENSE

I. THE FACTS

Your chances of getting robbed, raped, burglarized, assaulted, mugged, or murdered—or any combination of the above—are getting better all the time. And whether or not that assault is successful could depend greatly on how well prepared you are to defend yourself. Obviously you can't rely entirely on the police or on other outside help when there's no one else around—and sooner or later you may find yourself in that unfortunate circumstance when there's only you and the mugger, one-on-one. What do you do then?

If you are a skilled martial artist you have certain advantages over your adversary, despite the fact he may be armed. If you are versed in any method of self-defense, whether described in this book or not, you have a better-than-average chance of safely thwarting a mugging attempt. But if you are unfamiliar with any sort of systemized defense techniques, you're in trouble, your personal welfare is no longer in your hands. You are now a slave to fear.

Fear, as any martial artist will tell you, is the first thing a man must control when faced with such a threatening situation. Everyone is at least a little bit scared when threatened, especially by a weapon; there's that tightness in the stomach, the dryness in the mouth, the embarrassing, yet very real need to urinate; there's the nausea, the sweaty palms and underarms as the adrenalin surges through the body, pushed with hysterical urgency. Obviously it's virtually impossible to act in any positive manner when gripped by any or all of those symptoms. By allowing fear to rule the situation you add that much more to your opponent's arsenal. But by resisting the urge to panic, by relaxing rather than petrifying your muscles, you not only take away a weapon from him, you stand a fair chance of putting him on the defensive, at least psychologically. "People who are truly confident of their abilities," a Judo instructor has said in a policeman's training manual, "who have an inherent pacific security about themselves, exude such to those they meet. This can be a deterrent in many instances. But speed is also essential and, when coupled with that show of composure, your opponent will not only sense your confidence, he will see manifest before him that you obviously know what you're about." By rejecting fear you retain control, and by being in control of your emotions you give yourself the opportunity to play the situation by ear.

In some instances it might be better to feign cowardice, rather than offer an open challenge—in which case you might catch your opponent by surprise. Surprise is without a doubt a most formidable weapon and practically the only positive element an unarmed victim has to set up his adversary for subsequent defensive maneuvers. Without the element of surprise there's just no way an unarmed man can escape injury or possible death at the hands of an armed and determined aggressor—Hollywood, television, and various theatrical fantasies notwithstanding.

Occasionally a display of aggression on the part of the victim will deter a halfhearted mugger, but most senseis agree that if you challenge a determined would-be assailant, if you tip your hand that you are willing and able to fight, you automatically shift the odds in his favor, for you are putting him on his guard; you are letting him prepare himself. And, more importantly, you are taking away the element of surprise and without that, his *real* weapon, that knife or gun looms even larger and more threatening than before. He may decide to cut you a little just to "teach you a lesson." You may scare him with your overt challenge and rejection of his demands, but you may "scare" him to the point of panic or decisive action. Remember, *he* has the weapon, and a gun or a knife can inflict much more damage than a mere fist. There's nothing quite like seeing your own blood ooze out of you!

One other point on which all martial artists agree—indeed, all law enforcement officers to a man advise: If the perpetrator is armed and demands only your personal possessions, give them up without a struggle. Obviously there are no concrete ways to determine whether or not the assailant will not harm you even though you've willingly submitted to him, but at least give him the *opportunity* to leave you unmolested. If he elects to harm you anyway, then you can put into action whatever self-defense techniques you've mastered. It's a point above all others that cannot be overemphasized: *Don't offer resistance if the mugger is armed.*

"An ounce of prevention is worth a pound of cure." You've heard it a thousand times, but if you have to repeat it to yourself a thousand times more in order to remember its obvious wisdom, it's well worth the small effort. That axiom is nowhere more applicable than in a situation that doesn't have to be. If you don't *have* to be alone—after dark in a neighborhood noted for its high crime rate—then don't be. If you don't *have* to walk down a particular street under the same circumstances then don't. If you don't *have* to get into an elevator with one or more suspicious-looking characters already inside, or waiting to enter with you, then don't. Don't walk close to buildings late at night, past darkened doorways where a lurking mugger need only reach out and haul you in. Walk close to the curb. A little common sense in most circumstances can go a long way toward making life a little less dangerous. Don't give a mugger a better break than he already has. Some form of self-defense will give you the mental as well as the physical ability to not only react appropriately under given circumstances but to recognize and avoid obvious danger signals. Combat is emotional as well as physical, and good coordination between spirit, mind, and body is absolutely essential to good execution of techniques. This comes only with disciplined and prolonged study.

II. YOUR DEFENSE

Each individual should select those methods of self-defense that are easiest, that is, the most natural for him to perform. The idea is not to conquer difficult methods simply to show that you can do it, but to do one thing so well that it becomes second nature after a while, a reflex action requiring no thought and wasting no time.

Interestingly enough, most martial arts experts have favorite throws and holds that they use approximately 90 percent of the time. They teach many, many more, but they always revert to basics when asked their favorite techniques. Therefore a man need not be an *expert* in a complete style of martial art; he need only know the very basics and become *expert* in them.

John Kuhl, 6th Degree Black Belt in the Goju system of Karate, teaches a unique form of self-defense called Combat Karate. As the name suggests, the situation is combative—not sporting, and not necessarily artistically pleasing to the eye, but effective techniques that work. It's a no-nonsense, straightforward system that might well have as its motto ''the shortest distance between two points is a straight line,'' for that's exactly what it advocates. It gets from one point to another as quickly as possible and without any fanfare whatever. It's not a ''different'' or ''modified'' version of any one system, it's simply Karate with none of the frills, none of the eye-pleasing but time-consuming whirl-around, high-jumping, twisting and spinning, back-kicking techniques. John Kuhl doesn't see the street as a sporting arena or as a circus where paying customers get to see the greatest throw on earth. It's where life and death to him are very real—and death, especially, very permanent.

Sensei John Kuhl, who operates the Combat Karate Academy at 231 East 86th Street in New York, is also a sergeant in New York's Auxiliary Police Force, and instructs fellow patrolmen in his system of self-defense. He has been cited numerous times for bravery during his job and while off-duty. At this writing he has been nominated to receive the city's highest award for valor, having saved a Transit Authority Policeman from certain injury, possible death at the hands of an assailant. The street is John's job—knowing who is on it, what he's carrying, and what he's capable of doing with it is not only an integral part of that job but also an imperative one if he wants to stay alive and healthy!

As Sensei Kuhl well knows, two of the most commonly used weapons in a mugging attempt are: a knife, especially when only one person is being mugged, and a gun, usually when two or more victims are to be covered.

"If you're facing a knife or a gun, especially a gun," Sensei Kuhl says, "give him anything he wants. You're better off not taking any chances." However, if escape is impossible and the very real threat of injury imminent, action must be taken. "Try to put your man off-balance, then. Not by verbally challenging him, but by coming on like a coward, 'Please don't hurt me, please . . . ' By making him think you're afraid, you may get him to relax his initial intentions. He may break concentration thinking what a coward you are, and leave himself wide open for a surprise attack. He's probably cocky to begin with. After all, he's got the gun and he's apt to believe even a phony act of cowardice.

"Also, he's scared, too. He doesn't want to get caught, doesn't want to go to jail. He's got his own kind of fears. He's probably very nervous about the whole thing, especially if he's not an old-timer at the game. Chances are good, also, that the guy is unsure of his weapon, if it's a gun. First of all, unless he's a law officer or belongs to a rod and gun club, he doesn't get to practice with it very often, if at all. He may not know how to handle it; the weight, the size, the trigger action are likely to be new to him—perhaps he bought it specifically for this job—that possibility can be turned to your advantage."

III. THE BEST MOVE

There are admittedly few advantages when facing a gun, but those that do exist should be capitalized on. Obviously you can't do anything if the man is standing out of striking range, i.e. beyond arm's length. He can pull the trigger a lot faster than you can lunge at him. You must, if your life is threatened, bring him into proximity. A victim's best chances are when the gun is actually touching his body, for that is when the gunman is most vulnerable to a self-defense technique.

A gunman approaching a victim from behind usually places the barrel of the gun against the side of the victim on which he's holding the gun. That is, a right-handed gunman would normally shove the gun into the right kidney area of his victim—*normally!* However, a cautious gunman might place the gun cross-side—that is, his right hand with the gun pointed at his victim's left side. This is a distinct disadvantage for the victim because he assumes the gun is in the hand on the side it's touching; bad assumption. When the victim whirls and blocks at the gun hand, it takes a precious split-second longer to make contact, because he's pivoted toward the side where he thought the gun was. The unfortunate surprise is on him!

The smart, experienced gunman who's taking no chances in case you decide to get brave, might also place his *finger* in your back, holding the gun in his other hand, away from your body. When you make your move to strike at the gun hand, whirling and blocking, you'll have hit his *finger* hand, leaving the gun hand free to fire away. It's possible to determine if he's holding a finger or a gun against you only if there's a window or some other reflective surface exposing his position. Or, if he reached around with his free hand to search you, the gun, if there is one, is obviously in the other hand. Otherwise there is just no way to tell a finger from a gun in this situation.

There is such a thing as grabbing the gun itself when defending against an attack. As John Kuhl points out: "If you've seen the gun and recognize it as a revolver, you can prevent its being fired by grabbing the drum. Or, if it's an automatic and you're fast enough and *accurate* enough to slip any part of your hand between the hammer and the firing pin, all well and good—again, the gun won't fire. However, these techniques are extremely difficult to execute, especially the one with the automatic."

The best percentage move, according to John Kuhl, is to grab the *area* of the gun, the wrist, preferably, or the clothing at the wrist. And once you've got it, hold on to it for dear life, firmly, locking it so that it can't rotate back onto you. If you should catch the gun itself, hold as you would the wrist, *away from you,* or, if you can wrestle it so, pointed back at him. Sensei Kuhl cautions that almost inevitably the gun will fire at least once during the struggle. Don't let its sound scare or stun you into inaction!

IV. DEFENSE AGAINST THE KNIFE

If you can accept it as a lesser of two evils or can find some consolation in the fact, it is often easier to defend against a knife than a gun. First of all, the knife fighter must come into proximity in order to give meaning to his threat, unless of course he's expert at throwing the knife; few are. And, as with the gunman, the closer the attacker is the better your chances of safely defending yourself. However, if there's distance between you when the threat is made, the only common sense thing to do is to lengthen that distance. Run! Just as far and as fast as your legs can carry you. If you don't have to confront that knife, don't!

A man not necessarily skilled in the art of knife fighting—and make no mistake about it, it is an art—can be easier to handle than a gunman, but extra caution has to be taken lest nervousness or just plain carelessness cause him to cut you accidentally. A dope addict in desperate need of a fix is a typical case. He doesn't use a gun because he's probably more afraid of it than you are; he's not skilled with a knife but it's easier for him to handle and he quite likely gets a certain psychological strength from it; he's mentally and physically out of shape and without the knife would be little or no threat; he really doesn't have the "heart" for violence, for a confrontation—he wants only his fix without any trouble whatever. He's the guy most likely to cut you accidentally than any other. Absolutely unpredictable in his desperation, he may cut you whether you give him your money or not; he may "see" aggression where it doesn't exist; may "feel" aggression where complete acquiescence is offered. But because of these ambiguities good defense techniques could disarm him fairly easily.

It's the *skilled* knife fighter that is the toughest to defend against, sometimes even more so than a gunman. His mind and reflexes are generally as sharp as his weapon and he's not apt to be careless. A gunman, for instance, cocky and overconfident because of the nature of his weapon, doesn't really have to come close to his victim—but he does, putting himself in a degree of jeopardy because he's not used to in-fighting. But the knife fighter is. He's forced to work at close range, and if he's learned his art well, he's devastating. Unlike the gunman, he can practice anywhere at just about anytime, silently. He can conceal his weapon better and has less fear about being discovered. He can use his knife without drawing undue attention to himself. Times are too numerous where victims reported later that they didn't even realize they had been cut until after the mugger had fled!

Against a knife fighter John Kuhl warns: "You must know what you're doing. It only takes one mistake and you're going to have a knife between your ribs and the guy is going to fly away. In order to learn your holds, your punching and kicking techniques, you've got to work on them, go over them one hundred, two hundred, three hundred times. It's got to come like second nature: Someone attacks you, your block comes up, your counter comes right after—second nature. You have to do it before you even think, and you only get it through practice, repetition, repetition, repetition. I can't emphasize that enough. You practice it until it comes automatically."

"There are probably fifteen or twenty ways of getting out of a sticky knife situation," Sensei Kuhl says, "but some may only work for tall people, some for short, others for fast or slow people—and many are a bit on the fancy side; they look good in Hollywood but are totally impractical in real life. The techniques illustrated here are techniques that *work*. They're basic techniques. It doesn't matter if they're pretty or not as long as they get the job done."

Before even considering the following illustrations, John once more advises, "Avoid the situation at all costs. If you can get out of it by simply giving up your money, do so. Avoid the physical confrontation. Remember, once you're cut or shot, there's nothing that can be done to reverse matters. And getting cut is a helluva lot different than just getting punched. Getting punched is one thing; it may hurt, you may be able to weather it, absorb it even though painful. But once you're cut with a knife it's a whole new thing. There's blood—yours—and a great deal of pain and, even more importantly, fright. Your reaction to it cannot be determined. You more than likely won't be able to shake it off as readily as a punch or a clubbing. Whether it's only a flesh wound in the shoulder or on the arm, or a slash on the cheek, it's still your blood. If you can avoid spilling it, do."

In an unavoidable confrontation with a knife fighter, Sensei Kuhl advises: "The best time to make your move is when the knife first touches you, before he gets settled into going about his business. Because by then he'll be consciously leaning against you, pressing on the knife against your throat to make sure you don't make any sudden moves while he's searching for your money. This minimizes, if not actually prevents, your chances to defend successfully."

John says also that the victim must keep in mind that no matter what moves he makes, the chances are good that he's going to suffer some kind of cut. While the barrel of a gun might brush against the victim as the arm is blocked and the bullet spent in midair, it won't cause any injury. The blade of the knife though, will cut under the same circumstances. But if the techniques are executed properly, the cuts will be superficial.

"The moves have to be swift, crisp, and sharp," Sensei Kuhl says. "And the blows and kicks have to be hard driving forces. Once you've grabbed that wrist, hold it fast, immobilize it so that it can't turn the knife back onto you—and don't let go until he's dropped it or you can safely take it away from him."

The illustrations which follow, it should be noted, are just that—*illustrations*. *They are not instructions.* They make no attempt to persuade the reader that these techniques will work for him. They are illustrations of techniques that Sensei John Kuhl, after more than fifteen years of practice, feels are right for him. "You can't attempt to copy any illustrations depicting defense techniques," Sensei Kuhl says, "especially where weapons are concerned. You can't learn self-defense from a book, this or any book. It can help to augment study, but it can't replace it. You must practice, practice, practice—and then practice some more before even thinking of trying these techniques in an actual necessity. Remember, in real life, whatever you elect to do *has* to work. You get no second chance.''

Assisting Sensei John Kuhl in the following illustrations are his students at the Combat Karate Academy: Michael G. Goetz, Brown Belt, 3rd Kyu, and Bob Samuelson, 2nd Degree Black Belt.

DEFENSE AGAINST A GUN

ONE MUGGER—VICTIM STANDING—FROM BEHIND

1. In this situation, Michael, acting as the mugger, approaches from behind and presses the gun against Sensei John Kuhl's right kidney area.

2. John, in one swift and simultaneous movement, bends his knees and pivots to his right, into the gun. His arms, already raised on instructions from the gunman, swing down, his right arm striking the wrist of the gun hand, causing the gun to discharge into midair. If the blow is hard enough, the gun could conceivably go flying—but don't rely on it.

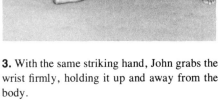

3. With the same striking hand, John grabs the wrist firmly, holding it up and away from the body.

4. This exposes the mugger's ribs and solar plexus for the roundhouse kick that Sensei Kuhl elects to throw.

5. John maintains his firm hold on the mugger's arm as the kick is executed.

6. A driving punch into the mugger's ribs follows.

7. Again, the gun hand is still firmly grasped by John.

8. Next comes a chopping *(shuto)* strike to the elbow.

9. Struck hard enough, the elbow will break.

10. If the gun has not been dropped by this time, this last technique will insure that result.

Under no circumstances should the gunman be allowed to fall to the ground free of the victim's grasp with the gun still in his hand. If it hasn't been dropped, it should be taken from him. If these techniques are executed properly with sufficient force, it's unlikely that he will be able to absorb them and merely feign unconsciousness. However, where weapons are concerned, no chances should be taken.

DEFENSE AGAINST A GUN

ONE MUGGER—VICTIM STANDING— FROM FRONT

11. A gunman who approaches from the front must be drawn into striking range, the closer the better. The best situation is to have the gun touching the victim. If the victim then reacts quickly, the mugger will not be able to fire the gun until after the victim has maneuvered out of harm's way.

Here the gunman confronts John, the victim, and has him raise his arms.

12. This enables John to pivot quickly clockwise and simultaneously swing his left hand down to grab the gun wrist and force it away from him—a much safer move than simply striking at the gun hand. Since his thumb is the only support on the underside of the mugger's wrist, John's hold is very temporary and he must act swiftly.

158

13. Immediately he throws a left-foot side thrust kick to the man's exposed ribs.

14. This move completed, John must continue to act quickly.

15. A straight hard punch to the temple follows.

16. The mugger should be effectively incapacitated at this point.

DEFENSE AGAINST A GUN

TWO MUGGERS—VICTIM STANDING— FROM FRONT

17. Usually in a situation like this the man in front will have the gun for his victim to see and fear. He might stand a foot or so away, menacingly, while his partner does the searching.

With Bob assisting as the partner, Mike points the gun at John's midsection, again instructing him to raise his hands.

18. John pivots instantly, reaching out with his right hand and grabbing and pushing the gun away from him.

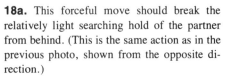

18a. This forceful move should break the relatively light searching hold of the partner from behind. (This is the same action as in the previous photo, shown from the opposite direction.)

19. If the partner is situated on the left side of the victim, the move will also position him in the direct line of fire. But don't depend on it. Sensei Kuhl doesn't.

20. His follow-up action is to throw a round-house kick to the gunman's solar plexus.

20a. Here we see this move from the front.

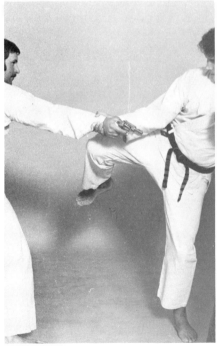

21. This kick completed, the partner must now be dealt with immediately.

22. Still holding the gun hand, which affords him some leverage, John shoots a roundhouse kick to the partner's groin.

23. The partner doubles in pain.

24. Quickly John grabs the gun with his left hand.

25. His right hand is now released for a devastating hammer blow into the elbow.

26. By pushing down with the left hand on the gunman's hand and wrist at the same time, the blow would probably break the gunman's elbow.

27. A straight punch to the temple of the partner, who is still doubled over from the groin kick, follows.

28. This should wrap things· up nicely.

167

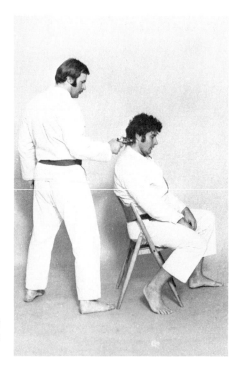

DEFENSE AGAINST A GUN

ONE MUGGER—VICTIM SEATED—
FROM BEHIND

29. Seated, on a park bench perhaps, a mugger approaches from behind and presses a gun against the back of John's neck.

30. If he instructs the victim to raise his hands, all the better, for that merely puts them closer to where they're going anyway.

168

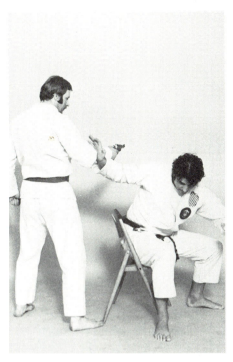

31. In one swift motion John twists in his seat, ducks his head and throws his right hand in a chopping *(shuto)* strike at the gunman's right hand.

32. His hand grabs at the clothing on the gunman's arm as John stands.

33. He then throws a quick side thrust kick into the man's ribs.

34. The mugger is pulled into the kick to double the force of the blow.

35. John then pivots around behind the mugger.

36. At the same time he grabs the gun wrist firmly with his right hand and throws his left arm around the gunman's neck.

37. The gun arm is braced across John's chest in an arm bar which, with just a little pressure, would enable John to easily break the mugger's arm. His left arm is positioned so that the wrist bone applies added pressure on the gunman's Adam's apple, a very effective hold. This could render the man unconscious.

DEFENSE AGAINST A GUN

ONE MUGGER—VICTIM SEATED—FROM FRONT

38. This time the mugger approaches from the front and has John raise his hands while pointing the gun at his head.

39. John elects to throw an inside block with his left hand.

172

40. He catches and holds the gunman's wrist firmly.

41. Immediately he is on his feet.

173

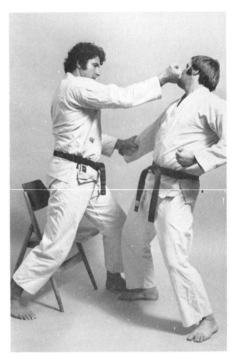

42. In one continuous flow, John completes the act of getting up with a hard straight punch to the gunman's face.

43. This is followed quickly with a striking choke hold.

44. At the same time he positions his right leg behind the attacker's left leg.

45. A mere push forward with the right hand will result in a takedown.

175

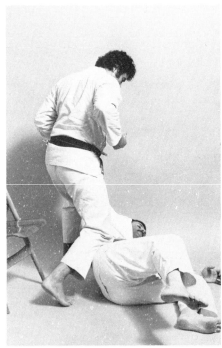

46. As the mugger falls John maintains his firm grasp on the gun hand.

47. A straight punch to the temple quickly follows before the attacker can react.

48. John continues to hold the gun hand even as the punch is executed. Once this move is completed John can safely remove the weapon from the man.

49. The victim has successfully extricated himself from another potentially dangerous situation through the expert use of Combat Karate.

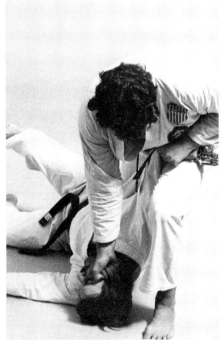

DEFENSE AGAINST A GUN

TWO MUGGERS—VICTIM SEATED—FROM FRONT

50. Here Mike stands in front of his victim, gun raised to fire point-blank at his face. Bob is situated behind and to the left of Sensei Kuhl, just beginning to go through his pockets for money.

51. With hands raised, John quickly brings his left hand down striking hard and grabbing at the gunman's wrist, catching the clothing.

52. Pushing the gun hand forward and leaning his body away from the direction in which the gun is pointed, John leaps to his feet.

53. As he does, he throws a *shuto* to the ribs of the surprised partner.

54. He then turns his attention immediately back to the gunman, switching grasps on the gun.

55. His freed left arm then moves up with an elbow strike to the chin/throat area. The gun arm meanwhile is stretched across John's chest in an arm bar with enough pressure applied to either force him to drop the gun or to break the arm.

DEFENSE AGAINST A KNIFE

ONE MUGGER—VICTIM STANDING—FROM FRONT

56. Bob Samuelson, acting as mugger, orders John to raise his hands.

57. The knife blade is pressed against John's jugular vein.

58. Sensei Kuhl quickly turns his head toward his right, at the same time bringing his left arm down.

59. He grabs and pushes away the knife wrist.

60. The move has placed victim and mugger side-by-side, knife arm extended and ribs exposed.

61. A swift side thrust kick follows.

62. The kick will probably cause him to drop the knife. If not, however, still grasping the wrist, a straight punch to the temple will accomplish that end.

63. At this point, the attacker is effectively put out of commission.

DEFENSE AGAINST A KNIFE

ONE MUGGER—VICTIM STANDING—
FROM BEHIND

64. The mugger approaches from the rear in this instance and presses his knife against the victim's left jugular vein.

65. Sensei Kuhl's first move is to tuck in his chin quickly, while dropping to a semisquat position.

66. An elbow strike is thrown immediately into the attacker's solar plexus. Under this kind of attack, the victim almost has to get cut if he offers resistance, but the cut, if the chin is tucked in and the semisquat executed correctly, will be on the chin or lower cheek rather than on the more vulnerable throat.

67. The mugger will almost instinctively squat with the victim, which is advantageous because his whole body is being forced to move and his concentration would more than likely shift from his knife hand to the unexpected reflex action. Before he can recover, the elbow strike is thrown to stun him, at least momentarily. Even if it misses its mark, it gives the victim precious time to grab the knife hand at the wrist with the same hand used to strike.

68. The knife can then be driven away from the victim's body.

69. This move is reinforced by a strike-grab with the left hand.

70. John now has a firm grasp on the knife hand and can concentrate on his following moves.

71. He then delivers a crisp *shuto* to the attacker's neck.

72. The attacker is effectively put out of commission.

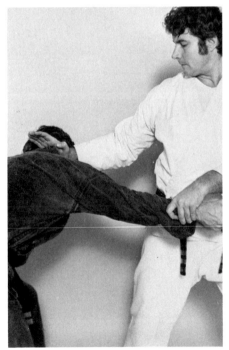

73. John's final move is a hammer blow/*shuto* to the back of the elbow.

74. This will break the arm and/or force release of the knife.

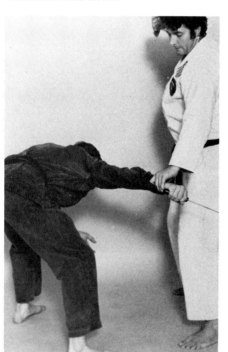

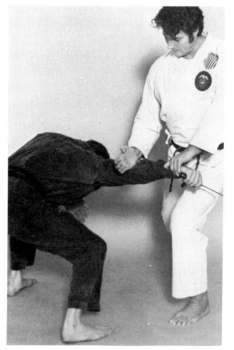

DEFENSE AGAINST A KNIFE

ONE MUGGER—VICTIM SEATED—FROM FRONT

75. Seated on a park bench, a subway train, or under some such similar circumstance, the mugger points the knife directly at the neck/face area of his victim.

76. This time Sensei Kuhl jerks his head back, away from the knife point, and throws an inside block to the man's arm.

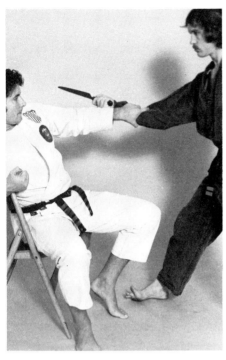

77. He grabs the knife wrist at the same time.

78. The closest point for contact is the man's groin, consequently a quick front thrust kick is thrown there.

79. This doubles the man over.

80. The mugger is now positioned perfectly for the knee smash that follows. Still holding the knife hand, Sensei Kuhl grabs the mugger by the head.

81. As he stands, John drives his knee upward.

82. The knee and the mugger's face, which John pushes downward with his right hand, meet in a forceful blow.

DEFENSE AGAINST A KNIFE

ONE MUGGER—VICTIM SEATED— FROM BEHIND

83. If approached from behind, as illustrated here, the victim has a slight advantage in that the mugger is already leaning over him, off-balance almost, and inclined to fall forward easily if pulled that way.

84. With his attacker semicrouched over him, knife at his throat, John tucks his chin in and grabs at the knife arm with both hands, twisting his body to the right toward his attacker.

194

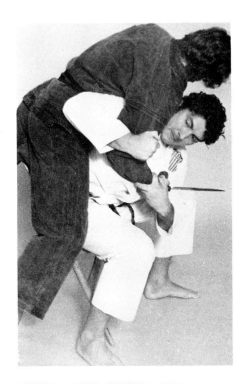

85. This move pushes the blade away from the danger area and, because of that "leaning" posture, the mugger is in perfect position for an over-the-shoulder toss.

86. John executes this move deftly.

87. The knife hand has remained in John's firm grasp all through the toss.

88. Once down, the mugger's ribs are exposed.

89. Taking advantage of this, John throws a straight punch to the ribs.

90. The mugger's arm, extended across John's left knee, could easily be broken merely by exerting pressure with the left hand.

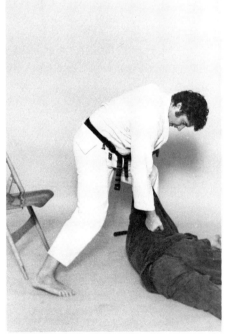

DEFENSE AGAINST A KNIFE

91. When working in pairs, chances are that at least one, if not both, of the muggers is inclined to be overly confident. They don't really expect resistance and their belief is further encouraged if their victim feigns submission—*convincingly*.

92. With the knife man pressing the blade against John's throat from behind and his partner beginning his search from the front, John quickly tucks in his chin, twisting neck and body in toward the knife man at the same time.

93. He grabs at the knife hand with both hands to get it away from his face and throat.

198

94. Once the hand is isolated, yet almost in the same split second, John throws a side thrust kick to the partner's solar plexus.

95. This should occupy him at least for the moment.

96. Turning his attention back to the knife man, John twists the elbow of the knife hand so that it is locked.

97. He then throws a hammer blow upward to break the elbow or at least force the release of the knife.

98. The partner receives a back kick into his midsection at this point.

99. John maintains his hold on the knife hand, just in case.

100–101. A backfist into the temple of the knife man follows.

102–103. And an elbow strike to the breast-bone for the *coup de grace*.

DEFENSE AGAINST A KNIFE

TWO MUGGERS—VICTIM STANDING—FROM FRONT

104. This time the knife man is facing John and the partner is ready to search from behind.

105. John blocks the knife hand forward with his left hand, grabbing and securing the wrist firmly.

106. He throws a crisp, straight punch, jablike, to the man's face to momentarily freeze him.

107. Then follows a backfist to the temple area of the partner behind.

108. This should stun the partner as well.

109. With the attacker's wrist firmly grasped, John throws a quick roundhouse kick to the solar plexus of the partner.

110. With the partner out of the way, John can now return to the attacker.

111. He does this with repeated shutos to the knife man's neck.

112. This is continued until the man is subdued and the knife retrieved.

DEFENSE AGAINST A KNIFE

TWO MUGGERS—VICTIM SEATED—FROM BEHIND

113. Once more in a park bench situation, John is approached from behind by a mugger with a knife and from the front by a partner ready to search him for money.

114. His first move is to grab and pull the knife hand away with his right hand.

115. Quickly, he throws a backfist to the partner's face, catching the bridge of the nose area which will cause temporary tearing, blurriness, and probably draw blood.

116. Next, a back kick to the groin.

117. In one continuous movement, using the man's wrist and extended arm for support, John changes feet and prepares to deal with the knife man.

118. He accomplishes this with a roundhouse kick delivered with his right foot to the knife man's solar plexus.

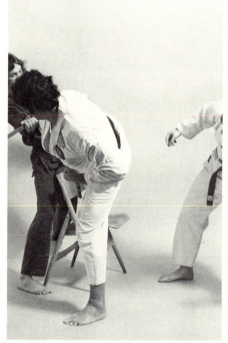

119. Then John quickly grabs the knife arm with his left hand and pulls down.

120. By throwing a hammer blow upward with his right arm the elbow should break and the knife be released.

DEFENSE AGAINST A KNIFE

TWO MUGGERS—VICTIM SEATED—
FROM FRONT

121. With the knife man situated in front, knife pointed at his victim's stomach, the partner begins his search from behind.

122. John elects to block the knife hand forward.

123. He grabs the knife man's clothing at the wrist and pushes the weapon away from his body.

124. At the same time John throws an elbow strike into the groin of the partner.

213

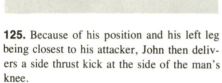

125. Because of his position and his left leg being closest to his attacker, John then delivers a side thrust kick at the side of the man's knee.

126. This will result in a takedown.

127. Still grasping the wrist, the next move could be a straight punch to the face.

128. Accompanying the punch could be a knee drop to the groin, and the assailants are again successfully vanquished.

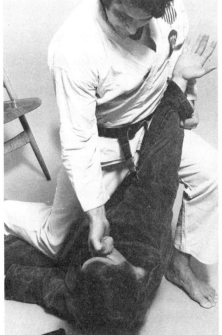

SELF-DEFENSE FOR WOMEN

I. WOMEN AND PHYSICAL COMBAT

Violence is naturally repugnant to most women. They will attempt to avoid it at all costs. Face-to-face physical confrontations are embarrassing, uncomfortable, unnerving. It isn't that they're incapable of aggression. When defending a loved one—a child, a husband, a parent, perhaps—a woman can be an absolute hellion, daring things undreamed of, performing feats near inhuman. She will respond to the needs of others instinctively, without fear or second thought—and of course, without form or design. Her moves are reflex actions: animal and uncontrolled.

Under controlled circumstances, that is, when competing against one another in a test of physical strengths such as boxing, wrestling (exceptions to the rules acknowledged—and women wrestlers are definitely exceptions), women have no "feel" for a fight. They have no ritualistic tendencies to prove their physical prowess. There is no real inner urge to "have it out" as with men. A man will give or take a bloody nose with matter-of-factness, almost hereditary resignation; a woman will usually settle for a catty remark.

This is not to say that women aren't competitive. On the contrary. There's no denying the competitive excellence of Suzanne Lenglen, Gertrude Ederle, Amelia Earhart, Babe Didrickson Zaharias, Althea Gibson, or Billie Jean King, just to name a mere handful of the many luminaries who at no time lost any of their femininity in the successful pursuit of their goals. But their mode of competition did not require "physical" combat—confrontation, yes, but combat, no.

216

But that was yesterday, before women's lib, equal rights, and the mushrooming popularity of a relatively new and exciting system of self-defense called "martial arts." The art itself began to instill a kind of pride. There was equality in the dojo, if not in actual physical strength, certainly in dedication of purpose. When allowed to compete with and against men, women showed a singularly unique ability to adapt and adjust to physical, mental, and spiritual rigors that had hitherto not been demanded of them. They did have, after all, a "feel" for the fight; they could and would toss, karate-chop and groin-kick a man without hesitation and with authority. And they would lose none of their femininity in the process.

One of the men most responsible for a major increase in the popularity of martial arts for women is Ed Kaloudis, 6th Degree Black Belt in the Koekian style of Karate. Mr. Kaloudis, whose main dojo is headquartered at 1245 Main Avenue in Clifton, New Jersey, currently instructs in three colleges and four universities including Montclair State College, William Paterson College, and Bloomfield College, in Montclair, Paterson, and Bloomfield, New Jersey, respectively. Mr. Kaloudis also teaches coeducational Karate at the Fairleigh Dickinson universities in Teaneck and Rutherford, New Jersey. He was one of the first martial artists to teach in universities in the New York metropolitan area, beginning with a Judo and Karate class at New York University in 1958. The number of women he has instructed in the martial arts since then number well into the thousands.

II. APPLYING DEFENSE TECHNIQUES

Ed Kaloudis does not pander to femininity, to female equality, or to male chauvinism; he does, however, put things in a proper perspective. The art is constant, he has said; those who study it change. Therefore let the student study the art, don't subject the art to the student.

"If you approach it as a different discipline," he replied to the question of whether or not women in the dojo should be catered to, "you lose the total concept of self-defense. When a man defends himself, it's usually against another man. A woman, when she has to defend herself at all, will most probably have to defend against a man—so she had better learn as well as a man.

"However, the concept of approaching a woman [to teach her self-defense] is a little different from that of a man. She must be made aware of the advantages that exist when confronted by an opponent of greater physical strength. For example, when a man attacks a woman—and every man is a chauvinist in his own way—he knows that she is the weaker sex and that he doesn't have to apply as much strength to subdue her as he would if he were facing a man. So, psychologically he is not as prepared to defend himself. There are weaknesses in his attack. If a woman is smart enough, knows how to react to that situation, she could gain the upper hand. She could defeat him.''

Sensei Kaloudis acknowledges that there are times to ''give in'' to an attacker, times to scream, times to run—if the circumstances permit. There are times also when a weapon or some kind of deterring instrument—a whistle or a flashlight, say—is appropriate for self-protection. But these are subject to variables and cannot always be relied on.

Avoiding the situation whenever possible is once more the paramount ''defense.'' Anything within reason that can be done to elude confrontation should be considered, Sensei Kaloudis contends. Also, once the crime is committed and the criminal gone, and the ''victim'' is safe, so to speak, leave well enough alone. ''If a man tries to steal a woman's purse . . .'' the sensei said, ''I'm not saying she should give it up. On the contrary, she should try as hard as she can to retain it. But, once he has the pocketbook in his possession—and now he's running away—if she decides to chase him and start screaming . . . well, suppose he has a gun? He's going to stop her from screaming. Is the money in the purse worth a life?

''Carrying a whistle inside your pocketbook is silly,'' Ed advises women. ''Outside your pocketbook is okay, along with any other kind of 'hidden' weapon, that is, a comb, scissors, hat pin, ball-point pen, etc. I personally don't advocate using anything other than your hands and feet, because by the time you open your pocketbook and find these 'weapons'—well, he's not going to just stand there waiting and watching, is he? However, if you are out alone late at night or early in the morning, on your way home, or about to enter the hallway of your home, or, about to enter the elevator and there's no doorman on duty, then I suggest you carry the weapon outside your pocketbook. You can carry it concealed in your hand. It could be a ball-point pen [steadied] between the index and middle fingers, braced against the palm. It can penetrate any given area of the body, the head, neck, chest, or stomach, if the man is not wearing a heavy outer coat. And you don't have to show the weapon. If he sees it he'll be prepared for it and that takes away the element of surprise. Under those circumstances it's fine to carry a weapon, but a woman must not depend on anything other than her own confidence and ability to defend against an attack.

''Most importantly a woman has to be mentally prepared for self-defense. If she is attacked, the first and foremost thing she must do is keep absolutely calm, tranquil. She must say to herself: 'I must not panic. I must think before I do anything else, and I must think first of all, What does it take for me to come out of this situation alive?' That's the most important thing.''

Attempted rape or robbery very often occurs in an elevator or other confined space—a narrow hallway, say, and Sensei Kaloudis remarks: ''A woman who is calm will make herself aware of the amount of space she has to 'work' in. She knows that certain techniques are not going to work, ones that require plenty of room to execute. So she concentrates on close combat techniques, knee and elbow strikes and so forth.

"A woman should never stand against the far wall in an elevator. She should stand close to the buttons so that, in the event she is attacked she could push the ALARM or STOP button. Even if she didn't get the chance to push them before he was upon her, she might push them accidentally in the course of the struggle. If she's away from them and the man is between her and them, obviously there's little chance at all.

"In order to be totally prepared for the attack, a woman should lean against the wall, one leg just resting lightly on the floor in readiness to kick out. With her shoulders braced against the wall for support and added strength, hands might be on hips or casually resting on the handrail if there is one. It's as natural-looking a stance as you'll see anywhere, yet the woman is in total readiness to repel any attack."

Out on the streets, many senseis advocate running—at least when the circumstance warrants it. If a woman feels she's being followed, they suggest she stop, turn, and face her "adversary." The crime situation what it is today, it could be a very real threat—or it could be her imagination. It may be nothing more than the neighbor from down the block returning with the quart of milk he'd forgotten on his earlier visit to the deli; someone walking his dog. But all agree that it's best not to take chances. If there's uncertainty on her part, cross the street and walk quickly but calmly in the opposite direction, they advise. She should run if she thinks she can outrun her would-be assailant, they say, or if she has a good headstart. She should run if there's refuge close by: a twenty-four-hour garage or deli, even the next block on which someone else might be walking who could conceivably come to her aid.

"By running," Ed Kaloudis says, "the environment changes and maybe she'll run into somebody who can save her. If the man is chasing her, yes, she should run. Or, if she has repelled an attack, if she has punched or kicked a man in the eye or the groin, she should not just stand there, she should run. But," Kaloudis cautions, "if she is caught, then she should calm down, go back to the first, most important attitude: don't panic! Don't put him in a frame of mind that forces him to knock you unconscious. If you're out cold you can't defend yourself. You can still be robbed, raped, still be killed. So calm down, think . . . 'what would be the best thing to do in this situation . . .'

"But when the woman is ready to act, when she has put the man off-guard, she should become explosive. She should yell and scream as loud as she can; this is the *kiai,* the screaming while she's hitting her opponent that gives her added strength. It develops the inner Chi, that surge that supplies the extra energy needed for adding power to her blows. And also, it scares the hell out of her opponent. One minute she was totally calm; the next she's like a raging volcano. She's hysterical, like a maniac. It shakes the man up.''

Robbing a woman of her money is one thing, rape is certainly another. The attacker's motives, his whole concept of approach is different. "If a man is going to rape a woman," Ed Kaloudis says, "he doesn't have it in his head that she is going to give in to him. He's expecting to be rejected. It would come as a total surprise to him if she expressed willingness, if she accepted and encouraged his advances. He's prepared himself for a situation that will require force, and if he has a knife at her throat or a gun at her head and she starts screaming, he's going to kill her. He's probably going to panic and kill her. What the woman has to remember is that his initial intentions are probably not to kill, but even if they were, he would kill her *after* the rape, not before. So she has time between the *now* and *then,* between his approach and the actual rape before death is considered on his part—unless, of course, she forces him to panic. She must get the man to be as relaxed as possible," Ed says, "get him to think she's enjoying what's happening; anything to put him off-guard. Then, when she's got him in a compromising situation—he can't rape her if both of them are standing there fully clothed!—when she senses that split-second opportunity to act, then those skills she learned at the dojo and practiced hour after hour should come to bear instinctively: where to grab, where to punch, to kick, scratch, etc.''

In order to maximize her chances of safely defending herself, a woman must know the most vulnerable points on the human body. These are those areas that, once struck with sufficient force, will afford her precious time to either run or follow up with repeated defensive maneuvers. But due caution must be taken for serious injury can be sustained, possibly death if the attack is formidable enough. Extra consideration, too, should be given each individual situation, and only the appropriate amount of force necessary to cope with it used. A desire for overkill could lead to a sticky legal situation, not to mention one's own personal regret. A mere annoyance, a man making only a nuisance of himself need not be rejected with a blinding two-finger stab to the eyes or a vicious kick to the groin. The primary objective here is on self-defense, not aggressive offense, and care should be taken when administering these techniques.

However, when actually confronted with a dangerous situation a woman must be able to defend herself effectively. "Avoid hitting muscular or fatty areas," Ed Kaloudis advises. "You can beat a man black and blue with blows to meaty areas, but he won't be black and blue until the next morning. By that time he'll have accomplished his goal. Look for bone or sensitive tissue.

"Also, twisting a man's hand or arm, turning back his wrist or bending his finger if he's stupid enough to extend one separated from the others and the woman is quick enough to grasp it, is a very difficult proposition. Men are strong, especially in their hands and wrists, in their arms. There are few women who can arm wrestle a man and win.''

There's nothing ''sporting'' about kicking a man when he's down, but then, there was nothing ''sporting'' about the way he attacked you to begin with—and kicking is exactly what Sensei Kaloudis recommends. ''Do not lean over to punch him once he's down,'' he warns, and the reasons should be obvious. ''Don't give him a chance to grab any more of your body than is necessary. Of course there will be times when a follow-up technique calls for a punch or elbow strike in order to insure speed and timing and to continue the flow of the offense, but once he's down the best techniques when possible are kicking techniques.''

Once again for the purposes of this book, it is emphasized that the following photographs are meant only as illustration of possible defense techniques. They are not to be construed as suggestions to the reader for his or her personal use. The techniques shown are defensive measures that Sensei Ed Kaloudis has selected as a guide to what might be done in the event of an attack.

Assisting Mr. Kaloudis in the illustrations showing the vulnerable parts of the body is his student, Denise M. Cram, Green Belt. In the illustrations of defense maneuvers Sensei Kaloudis' assistants are Joanne Ligosh, Brown Belt, and George Scordilis, First Degree Black Belt.

VULNERABLE POINTS ON THE BODY

1. *The Eyes*. Starting at the top, the most vulnerable points are the eyes. Hitting them with any sharp object, with the fingers stabbing, as illustrated here, or with the knuckles doubled into a backfist strike is a most effective technique. "However," as Sensei Kaloudis cautions, "that should be done only in dire emergencies—not when a person attempts to steal your pocketbook. You should not blind a human being because he happens to desperately want or need ten dollars out of your pocketbook. The eyes are very, very vulnerable."

2. *The Nose*. Hitting straight at the nose, or hitting down on it—*not up!* which would push the bone into the brain causing death or at the very least, irreparable brain damage—is an effective means of self-defense. A blow struck straight onto the nose would cause tearing or blurriness of the eyes. Here the victim strikes the attacker in the nose with the heel of her palm.

222

3. A backfist to the nose is just as effective, if not more so. A hard blow could, of course, break the nose and/or cause it to bleed, and sometimes just the sight of his own blood is enough to change the attacker's mind about further aggression.

4. *The Ears.* The ears are vulnerable to knuckle blows and thumbpoking. Here Denise applies quick hard thumb pokes to the mugger's ears.

5. Another very good technique is to cup both hands, as illustrated, and bring them down hard onto both ears simultaneously. This produces a dizzying effect. It could, in some cases, "pop" the eardrums and leave the assailant staggering.

223

6. *The Chin*. The chin is especially vulnerable to hard blows thrown from either side rather than straight on. Fist, forearm, ridge hand, and foreknuckle fist blows are effective. Here Denise demonstrates a hard backfist to the chin, stunning the attacker.

7. In this instance the victim uses a sharp elbow strike to the chin, an action that could easily result in a dislocated jaw.

8. A man with a strong neck might withstand a blow directed straight on to the chin. However, a front kick straight on is a different matter, and could nicely do the job.

9. *The Throat.* Women should not throw blows, karate chops, judo chops or whatever to the side of a man's neck. If he's got a strong neck he's going to withstand the blow easily. A useful move is a foreknuckle fist strike, with the first two phalanxes of the fingers bent in, sent straight into the Adam's apple, as pictured here. A clenched fist will do the job, too, but if the man's chin is tucked in there won't be room for it between chin and chest and the blow will be ineffective.

225

10. An elbow strike to the throat is an especially devastating blow.

11. A shuto to the throat, too, will have excellent results.

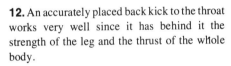

12. An accurately placed back kick to the throat works very well since it has behind it the strength of the leg and the thrust of the whole body.

13. Here the victim employs a thumb jab to the throat.

14. *The Ribs.* A hammer blow, as shown here, or a punch with the knuckles to the ribs works very well. Knuckles will find their way into the spaces between the ribs where the more tender areas are.

14a. This is a view of the hammer blow to the ribs from the rear. It takes a good deal of power to break a man's ribs, even with a hammer blow, so the woman shouldn't be overly concerned about holding back when hitting here. It's a good area to strike at (if he's not wearing a heavy outer coat) in a close situation.

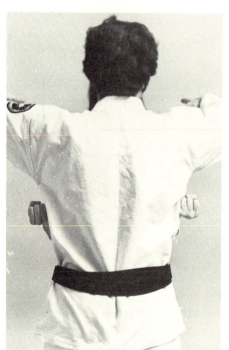

15. *The Solar Plexus.* This has to be a well-aimed blow, otherwise the woman might hit the man's chest or stomach, both of which may be well developed and able to absorb the shock. Here Denise accurately places a powerful back kick to the solar plexus.

16. This elbow strike to the attacker approaching from the rear would knock the wind right out of him, doubling the man over and rendering him prone to just about any kind of follow-up technique desired.

17. Another elbow strike, right on target to the solar plexus, this time from the side.

18. *The Groin.* This should be fairly obvious. Any blow—a punch, kick, knee, grasp, or squeeze action to the man's groin is going to cause considerable pain and anguish. At certain times a swift, powerful kick is the best method because it keeps you out of range of any "reaching" reaction the attacker might instinctively attempt.

19. In close combat the knee smash is super-effective, this one executed from the front. If necessary, a grabbing, squeezing, and pulling down hard of the testes is usually enough to make a man forsake his intentions.

19a. Here the victim uses a hard knee smash to the groin from the side.

20. *The Knee.* The knee is probably the most vulnerable area on the lower body. A solid kick there will cause a great deal of pain, could lock and break the knee if administered correctly and with sufficient force. Here the victim throws a kick at the back of the knee, simultaneously striking the chin with a palm heel blow. This maneuver is usually a part of a takedown technique and might be used merely to warn or embarrass a nuisance who won't take no for an answer.

21. Here Denise administers a painful side thrust kick to the side of the attacker's knee.

22. When positioned on the other side of the attacker, a side thrust kick to the inside of the knee is effective.

23. A combination technique that Sensei Kaloudis prescribes under certain close circumstances is a back kick to the knee, as shown here.

24. After the back kick, a scraping down on the sensitive shinbone and a final heel stomp on the instep provides a painful finish.

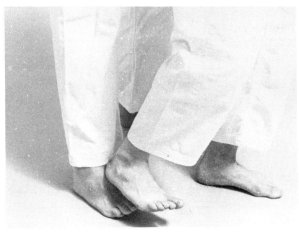

BREAKING A CHOKE HOLD
FROM THE FRONT—METHOD 1

25. There are two techniques that a man might employ when attempting to choke a woman. In this case George grabs Joanne around the throat and pushes her backward, as though to pin her against a wall.

26. Her first move is to take a *voluntary* step backward so she can regain her balance.

27. Then, turning her head to one side so she can get some breathing room, she twists her hips and torso counterclockwise. At the same time she brings her right arm up and around, close to his wrists.

28. Bringing her arm down hard, she can then force the attacker's arms down and away from her throat.

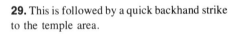

29. This is followed by a quick backhand strike to the temple area.

30. Attacker stunned, the victim can now make her escape or prepare to further defend herself.

BREAKING A CHOKE HOLD
FROM THE FRONT—METHOD 2

32. In this instance she grabs the man's hand tightly to prevent further choking and to give her a moment to breathe. She then quickly brings her knee up hard, smashing into his groin; this is not just a strike, it is a driving, forceful smash.

31. A different technique is required when a man attempts to choke the woman while pulling her toward him.

33. This should release the choke hold, at which point she's free to step back slightly and throw a front kick again into the groin.

34. Doubled in pain, the attacker is now in position for her next maneuver.

35. The victim follows with a powerful elbow strike to the back of his head.

36. This move is rendered doubly effective by bringing her knee up hard to meet his head as she strikes it.

BREAKING A CHOKE HOLD FROM BEHIND

37. As the man grabs her and attempts to push her forward, toward an alley, say, the woman should step forward ahead of the force if she can in order to regain her balance.

38. Then, as Joanne demonstrates, swiftly bring the right arm up and around. This will bring the attacker's hands together.

39. By bringing her arm down again quickly, the mugger's arms can be caught and locked.

40. Next Joanne throws an open palm to the nose. The blow is thrown while the attacker's head is facing down (photo #39), flattening the nose and pushing the head back.

41. This should at least stun the aggressor.

42. Immediately after this strike Joanne throws a straight punch to the groin.

43. Then a quick knee smash to the groin.

44. This devastating move is in accord with Sensei Kaloudis' suggestion: "Always change the striking area. If you strike high at first, try to make the second strike low, and vice versa. It confuses the opponent, keeps him off-balance. As well as the pain he's experiencing, he doesn't know where he's going to get hit next."

45. This advice is obviously very useful.

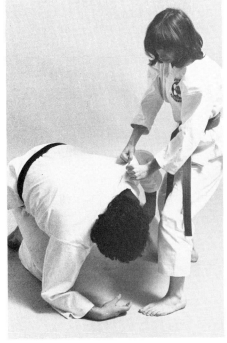

BREAKING A WRIST HOLD

46. "When the wrist is grabbed," Sensei Kaloudis says, "the first thing to do is to stabilize yourself with the person's hold. Use him as your support. In other words, it's as though he were giving you a third leg to stand on." With George grabbing and Joanne using him as her foundation, the next thing she does is take a half-step forward.

47. She then turns rapidly and throws a side kick at the side of his knee.

48. This should cause the knee to give way.

49. As her opponent is falling, Joanne follows with a hard backhand strike upward into the face.

50. Because the man is falling, his dead weight gives added strength to Joanne's backhand strike.

51. This whiplash technique could be enhanced with another strike.

52. Joanne chooses to throw a straight punch down into the groin.

BREAKING THE UNWANTED EMBRACE FROM FRONT

53. When a strong man grabs and squeezes a woman, locking her arms at her side, as illustrated, it is nearly impossible for her to match strengths. Any attempt to escape on her part will only make him squeeze tighter and prepare himself for a possible defense. However, if the woman doesn't panic, makes the man feel that his embrace is welcome, then she can catch him off-guard.

Here Joanne has relaxed her body, lets the man have his way, perhaps encouraging him with an embrace of her own, a kiss on the cheek, squirming seductively against him; anything to get him to relax. "That may sound repulsive to some women," Sensei Kaloudis acknowledges, "but it may also save their lives!"

54. Once he's relaxed, Joanne then grabs his clothing as though returning his passion, but in reality she's again using him as her foundation. He's taller and stronger and, lifted off the ground or up on her toes this way, she has no foundation of her own.

55. Now she is as one with him, and as he lifts her, using her hold on his clothing, Joanne brings her knee up hard into his groin, repeatedly.

56. That should force a release of his hold.

57. At this point the victim can then grab the attacker by the hair, who is doubled over because of the groin smashes.

58. Following through, she pushes his head down onto her knee that is again coming up hard to meet it.

59. The attacker, at this point, undoubtedly regrets his attempted embrace.

BREAKING THE UNWANTED EMBRACE FROM BEHIND

60. If a man embraces a woman from behind, again locking her arms at her sides, and tries to rush her forward, against a wall, say, he has to release the embrace, otherwise he pins his own hands against the wall. He's not going to ram her against the wall in this position. Also, if he pushes the victim close to a wall, a simple method of keeping away from it would be to just kick out with an extended leg against the wall, pushing him backward.

61. In any case, the important thing for the woman to do is to grab onto some part of his clothing, to again become as one with him, and to at least partially stabilize herself.

62. The man can't throw her down from this position, swing and carry on as he may.

63. He may try to flail her around to force submission.

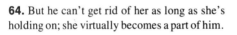

64. But he can't get rid of her as long as she's holding on; she virtually becomes a part of him.

65. From this vantage point a swift back kick to the knee would be the best move.

66. This is followed with a scraping down hard on the shinbone.

67. The woman shouldn't be afraid to be rough. After all, she's trying to escape.

68. Next, as shown here, a sharp stomp is delivered to the instep of the attacker's foot.

69. This stomp should be hard, applied with the heel of the foot. By this time the victim should be free of the man's embrace.

70. Before he can recover, a quick elbow strike is sent into the solar plexus.

71. Immediately following the woman throws a rapid backfist to the nose/eyes area.

72. And finally, a roundhouse kick to the groin. Again a whiplash effect has been employed, confusing the man and keeping him off-balance.

73. It's practically impossible to twist or turn the arm of an opponent who is taller and twice your weight—which is exactly what George is at 240 pounds! Joanne simply cannot win a tug-of-war with him.

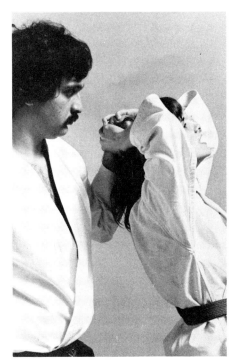 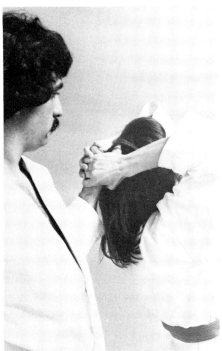

74. What she can do, though, is to grab and hold the hand that is clutching her hair.

75. By pushing down on his hand she can prevent further pulling and stabilize herself.

76. She then quickly spins her head and upper torso in toward him, lashing out at his knee at the same time with a side kick. This is an effective technique, but it's also to stun him momentarily, to inflict pain on him, to give him something other than your hair to think about.

77. That accomplished, Joanne then unleashes a swift back kick to the groin, after which she's free to turn in the right direction and run.

COPING WITH THE MOVIE AND SUBWAY MASHER—METHOD 1

78. Seated in a darkened theater, in an empty subway car, or on a park bench, a woman has several alternatives if approached by a masher: She can change her seat, scream for help or leave the premises. If these fail, she must stay and deal with the problem.

In this situation, seated side-by-side, Joanne has already removed George's hand from her thigh several times.

79. Seeing no way out and no one around to help her, she allows him to continue, touches him back, smiling at him to put him at ease.

80. She holds his arm "affectionately" with her left hand.

81. Still suspecting nothing, the masher suddenly receives a sharp shuto to the throat with Joanne's right hand.

82. He has been caught effectively unaware.

83. Then with that same hand, she grabs him by the hair.

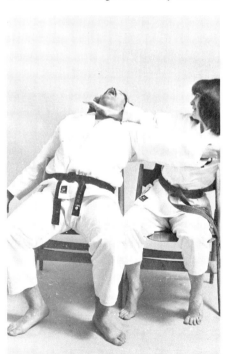

84. Standing, she rams his face down onto the seat in front, or, if on a park bench, she might throw a knee smash. And then, of course, she vacates the vicinity as quickly as possible.

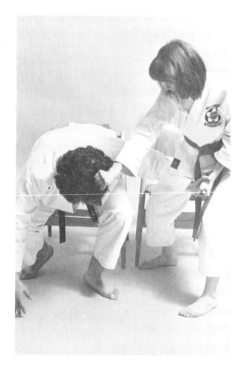

COPING WITH THE MOVIE AND SUBWAY MASHER—METHOD 2

85. Under the same circumstances a man might put his arm around the back of the woman's chair, onto her shoulders.

86. Again, after repeated rejections of his advances and with no alternatives, Joanne allows him to pursue his pleasure. She holds his hand, kisses and fondles it, all the while leaning closer as though snuggling up.

87. She's also cocking her elbow close to her side and under her left arm so that he can't detect her intentions.

88. She then lets loose with an elbow strike to the throat.

89. The movement has to be sure and quick, catching the masher with his guard down. The man is momentarily stunned and set up for Joanne's next move.

90. Quickly, she stands up.

91. Then she shoots.a straight punch down to the groin.

92. Since he is already doubled over, Joanne is able to grab him by the hair.

93. To finish, she forces his head down onto her knee smash.

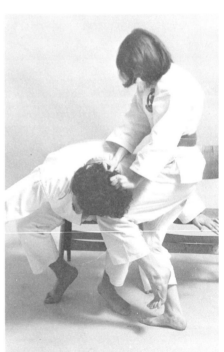

PREVENTING THE PURSE SNATCH

94. Most women today carry pocketbooks that have a shoulder strap, which are much harder for a thief to "snatch" than handbags. As a matter of fact, once a thief has pulled at her pocketbook, if the woman holds fast to the strap the tautness caused by the tug-of-war becomes her stabilizer; she can use that leverage to swing into any number of kicking techniques. Here George has already run past, grabbed at the pocketbook, and is attempting to wrest it from Joanne.

95. However, Joanne refuses to let go and steadies herself with the strap.

96. Swiftly she lashes out with a front kick.

97. Striking the side of his knee, Joanne effects a takedown.

98. On his way down she follows through with a hammer blow to the temple.

99. From there she's free to follow up with other techniques, or run.

THE ZEN MACROBIOTIC DIET

The traditional food of the Zen Buddhist monks of ancient Japan was macrobiotic in preparation. It purportedly enabled those holy men to be the healthiest and longest-lived people of that Far Eastern culture. As well as being superb martial artists, they were also consummate chefs. The kitchen was virtually sacred and only those of the highest order and most adept at food preparation were allowed within.

The monks were strict vegetarians; not only meat but fish, fowl, and dairy products were prohibited at their table. Rice, the brown, unpolished variety, was the main staple in their repertoire of food fare, and for good reason: it contained the perfect balance of Yin and Yang, the ancient Eastern philosophy of expansion and contraction. It was the perfect food, containing all the nutrients necessary for sustaining life.

Macrobiotic, literally translated from the Greek means "big" or "great life." It is also broken down to: *macro,* meaning great; *bio,* meaning vitality; and *biotics,* meaning rejuvenation. Zen macrobiotics, then, would be the very special art of selecting and preparing certain basic foods with an attitude for producing longevity and rejuvenation. The term Zen macrobiotic was coined by Sakurazawa Nyoiti, known to Westerners as George Ohsawa, long after the monks had established their way of preparing meals as a spiritual link for earthbound man to attain harmony with his metaphysical origin.

Zen macrobiotics today differs from the ancient practice by the holy men only in that it allows for modern man's having traveled so far afield of his beginnings, permitting some small amount of foods that are not normally associated with vegetarianism; fish and fowl, for example, are allowed as "secondary" foods. Also, strict Zen macrobiotic practitioners would not eat foods out of season nor those grown beyond an approximate five-hundred-mile radius of their home. However, because the "natural" order of eating has all but disappeared thanks to modern technological means of cultivating, processing, preserving, and distributing foods from all over the world to peoples all over the world, some concessions are made in the laws—but only for beginners and only as a means to the ultimate perfect balance of Yin and Yang.

Yin and Yang are the Chinese words for expressing "oneness" or "polarity" with the universe. All things contain Yin and Yang but not necessarily in perfect balance. Through macrobiotics constant effort is made to achieve that balance, to reach that level of oneness with the cosmos.

Yin is expansion; Yang contraction. The former has an outward, centrifugal tendency; the latter an inward, centripetal inclination. Yin is sugar; placed on the tongue it causes it to expand. Yang is salt; placed on the tongue it causes it to contract. By Western standards, Yin is acidity and Yang alkalinity. A formula for the two might be thus:

$$Yin = acid = potassium = sugar$$
$$Yang = alkaline = sodium = salt$$

For the body to be in a good state of health, a balance of Yin (acidity) and Yang (alkalinity) must be present, otherwise the body suffers various digestive disorders. And, what affects the stomach must eventually affect all other parts of the body, including, and especially, the brain. Excessive amounts of Yin, taken either through drugs high in acid or by food of equal acidic proportions, would cause expansion (or hallucination) of the mind. With drugs the process is quick; with food and/or drink it takes longer.

Philosophically, women are Yin, men Yang. A baby of either sex at birth is Yang—tiny and shriveled, contracted. As it grows it becomes more Yin. At death, it has again become contracted and Yin. Yin is passive, receptive; Yang, outgoing, stronger. Both seek each other continually in the way that opposites attract. Night—cool, dark, and less active—is Yin. Day—warm and energetic—is Yang. Winter—cold, reserved—is Yin. Summer—hot, extroverted—is Yang. In winter we tend to eat heavier, heartier Yang meals; in summer we prefer the green leafy Yin vegetables.

For good health our bodies should maintain an approximate ratio of five-to-seven parts potassium (Yin) to one part sodium (Yang). However, the average nonmacrobiotic diet includes great amounts of meat and sugar. While this is in effect some form of balance, the foods are extremes; meat is very Yang and sugar very Yin and they do not follow a rule of moderation paramount in Zen macrobiotic philosophy. The only sugar that is recomended in the macrobiotic diet is that which is extracted naturally from organically grown vegetables or grains; the simple act of chewing will produce a sugar from a starchy grain while it is still in the mouth. The policy against meat, fish, and fowl is primarily based on the concept that all nutrients come originally and naturally from the vegetable world. In this state they are nourishing and digestible. But, once digested they are altered. In the case of animals, they are usually fed chemically treated grains and vegetables, and they themselves are chemically treated with vaccines, hormones, antibiotics, fatteners, tenderizers, etc. Consequently animals break down and alter the balance of the nutritive elements of not only vegetables but themselves; they are anything but "natural." Fish, with the discoveries of polluted waters—whole oceans!—is falling more and more into disfavor.

Brown rice, as earlier mentioned, is the primary food. Within a single grain may be found all the nutrition a body needs for good health. In its original state, brown rice has seven layers or "skins." The outer layer is highly resistant to chemicals but physically it's very weak. Therefore great care must be used when husking. The recommended rice for Zen macrobiotic purposes is the organic, short-grained variety, carefully milled and, whenever possible, that which was recently picked (within three months!). In comparison to the "polished" white variety, brown rice contains approximately 25 percent more protein, is higher in calcium, silicium, magnesium, phosphorus, thiamin, riboflavin, and niacin. It is low in cholesterol and practically free of saturated fats. Rice is admittedly starchy; however, because of its low fiber content and elements in its outer layers, it is very easy to digest.

Among some of the other more prevalent items to be found in a macrobiotic diet are:

Aduki beans—very Yang in content, this Japanese cousin to the American cowpea is very high in protein. A small hard red bean with a white dot on the top, it has a unique flavor and is the most popular of all beans among practitioners.

Bancha tea—the most essential beverage in a diet that insists on little or no liquids most of the time, especially when eating. Undyed and pure, this Japanese green tea contains approximately three times the amount of calcium found in cow's milk. It is also believed to combat fatigue.

Bonito flakes—used mainly for flavoring soups, stocks, etc. They are the shavings of boned and over-dried bonito fish.

Buckwheat—a cereal plant with more than one hundred and fifty varieties growing in North America alone.

Bulgur—Near Eastern wheat that has been partially processed. Its sweet, somewhat nutty flavor makes it a favorite as a cereal.

Burdock—a long, thin root vegetable that is occasionally used to make tea. Also called "gobo," it grows wild throughout North America, and is said to aid sexual endurance.

Chestnut flour—a sweetener as well as a thickening agent made from ground chestnuts.

Daikon—Japanese white radishes, usually available dried, they are much stronger than the North American red variety.

Ginseng tea—made from the root of the ginseng plant, which grows abundantly in the eastern United States and throughout the world. Used often as a medicine, it purportedly has properties that will increase sexual desire and/or performance.

Gomasio—table condiment made from ground toasted sesame seeds and sea salt. Used in place of "commercial" salt.

Hiziki—black, stringlike seaweed with a particularly pleasing flavor.

Kasha—coarse, cracked buckwheat or millet; another name for buckwheat groats.

Kohkoh—a blend of grains and cereals ground into flour and used principally as a gruel for infants; also used in desserts.

Kuzu—a vegetable root gelatin used as a thickening agent much as arrowroot or corn starch; also used for medicinal purposes.

Miso—made by fermenting together soybeans, whole wheat, and sea salt for at least three years, this Japanese soybean "paste" is widely used for flavoring and because of its protein content. However, only those found in macrobiotic stores are recommended since the commercial variety contains additives.

Mu tea—Japanese herb tea made from ginseng and fifteen other medicinal plants. Reputedly has some medicinal qualities.

Nori—a purple seaweed that is available in thin sheets and need only be lightly toasted for consumption.

Sea salt—unrefined and unadulterated salt that is the result of evaporated sea water. Stronger than commercial table salt, it contains many trace minerals and iodine, but must be roasted slightly before using to eliminate excess chlorine.

Sesame butter—also known as *tahini,* this Near Eastern paste is made from ground sesame seeds.

Tamari—pure soy sauce made and extracted during the production of miso. Only those found in macrobiotic stores are recommended; commercial varieties contain additives.

Tofu—soybean curd made from the liquid in which soybeans have been crushed and softened. Solidified by boiling, it is available in most Oriental stores but can be readily made at home.

Udon—flat, hard Japanese wheat or cornmeal noodles similar to Italian vermicelli.

Umeboshi plums—plums aged and preserved in brine for at least eighteen months, but usually three years. Used primarily with vegetables and in salads.

Some of the laws of Zen macrobiotics are not unlike those which are practiced by nonmacrobiotic dieters. The idea of a well-balanced meal, which looks appetizing and contains all the nourishment necessary for one's well-being, is a commonsense principle that is shared by nearly everyone everywhere.

Coffee is taboo in the macrobiotic regimen, as are any of the commercially packaged teas that contain carcinogenic dye. Any "industrialized" food or drink; all fruits and vegetables not organically grown, out of season, or from a climate contrary temperature-wise to one's own is also prohibited. Drinking while eating is not advised, and when liquid is consumed, it should be taken in small sips and be neither too hot nor too cold. Hot spices are not recommended, although moderate amounts of garlic, ginger, bay leaf, basil, oregano, and thyme are all right for sprucing up a meal; cinnamon and vanilla bean are also allowed to accent a particular dish.

"You must chew your drinks and drink your foods," Mahatma Gandhi reportedly said. And in the Zen macrobiotic scheme of things it is practically a golden rule. Chewing exercises the facial muscles, breaks down the fiber content of the food to make digestion easier, and prevents, to a certain extent, overeating. When food is gulped down quickly, it is only after they are stuffed that people realize they were really full and could have stopped probably seven or eight mouthfuls earlier. Sipping and savoring liquids, "chewing" them, in effect, avoids that common bloated feeling also prevalent among those who drink too quickly, consequently too much.

A Zen macrobiotic diet is not overly strict. It does, in fact, seek to be as flexible as possible without breaking the cosmic philosophy on which it is founded. It does allow for man's imperfections to be gradually overcome in order to achieve the cosmic oneness. The desire for and eating of animal products is an indulgence that must be at least minimized, then, hopefully, totally eliminated. A mixed diet consisting of grains, fruits, vegetables, nuts, and beans can provide all the vitamins, minerals, sugars, starches, fats, and oils necessary for energy, for body-building, and tissue repair.

For the sake of a life free of earthly ills and for an easier path to harmony with the universe, it recommends only natural foods, untampered with and untainted by man. "You are what you eat," a noted nutritionist has said. You are Yin and Yang then, according to Zen macrobiotics. And if you are balanced in perfect proportion, you are at one with yourself and with your beginnings, and are in keeping with these words from the *Upanishad:* "[From food] verily, are produced all creatures—whatsoever dwells on earth. By food alone, furthermore, do they live, and to food, in the end, do they return, for food alone is the eldest of all beings, and therefore it is called the panacea for all."

APPENDIX A

BELT RANKINGS

Belt ranks in the martial arts differ from country to country, and from school to school. Each sensei, or teacher, may evolve his own color system, usually progressing from white to black, but the following are generally accepted rankings:

JUDO	SPORT JUDO
White	White
Green	Yellow
Brown	Orange
Black	Green
	Blue
	Brown
	Black
	Red & White

JAPANESE KARATE	KOREAN KARATE
White	White
Yellow	Yellow
Green	Green
Purple	Blue
Brown	Red
Black	Black

APPENDIX A

Belt rankings have not as yet been widely adopted in the disciplines of Aikido, T'ai Chi Ch'uan, and Kung Fu.

There are three possible degrees of Brown Belt and ten degrees of Black Belt. Each school or discipline may adopt the number of degrees in either belt that is best suited to its needs and standards. The full list of possible degrees is as follows:

BROWN BELT	BLACK BELT
Ikkyu —1st Degree	Shodan — 1st Degree
Nikyu —2nd Degree	Nidan — 2nd Degree
Sankyu—3rd Degree	Sandan — 3rd Degree
	Yondan — 4th Degree
	Godan — 5th Degree
	Rokudan — 6th Degree
	Shichidan— 7th Degree
	Hachidan— 8th Degree
	Kyudan — 9th Degree
	Judan —10th Degree

APPENDIX B

FOR FURTHER READING

Bartlett, E. G. *Judo & Self-Defense*. Arco Publications, 1962.

Cheng, Man-Ch'ing and Robert W. Smith. *T'ai Chi—The Supreme Ultimate Exercise for Health, Sport & Self-Defense*. Charles E. Tuttle Company, 1967.

Delza, Sophia. *T'ai Chi Ch'uan: An Ancient Way of Exercise to Achieve Health and Tranquility*. Cornerstone, 1972.

Dominy, Eric. *Judo: Beginner to Black Belt*. Wehman Brothers, 1974.

———. *Judo Techniques & Tactics*. Dover Publications, 1969.

Feng, G. and H. Wilkerson. *T'ai-Chi, A Way of Centering*. The Macmillan Company, 1969.

Freudenberg, Karl. *Natural Weapons: A Manual of Karate, Judo & Jujitsu Techniques*. A. S. Barnes & Company, 1962.

Gleeson, G. R. *Anatomy of Judo*. A. S. Barnes & Company, 1969.

Gruzanski, Charles V. *Spike & Chain: Japanese Fighting Arts*. Charles E. Tuttle Company, 1968.

Haines, Bruce A. *Karate's History and Traditions*. Charles E. Tuttle Company, 1968.

Harrington, Anthony P. *The Science of Judo*. Emerson Books, 1962.

Harrison, Ernest J. *A Manual of Karate*. Wehman Brothers, 1974.

Harvey, M. G. *Comprehensive Self-Defense*. Emerson Books, 1967.

Huang, Al C. *Embrace Tiger, Return to Mountain: The Essence of T'ai Chi*. Real People Press, 1973.

Hui-Ching, Lu. *T'ai Chi Ch'uan: A Manual of Instruction*. St. Martin's Press, 1973.

Maisel, Edward. *Tai Chi for Health*. Holt, Rinehart & Winston, 1972.

Mattson, George E. *The Way of Karate*. Charles E. Tuttle Company, 1963.

Nakae, K. *Jiu Jitsu Complete*. Wehman Brothers, 1974.

Parker, Edmund K. *Secrets of Chinese Karate*. Funk & Wagnalls, 1968.

Plee, H. D. *Karate: Beginner to Black Belt*. Wehman Brothers, 1967.

Shioda, Gozo. *Dynamite Aikido*. Translated by Geoffrey Hamilton. Wehman Brothers, 1969.

Tegner, Bruce. *Bruce Tegner Method of Self-Defense: The Best of Judo, Jiu Jitsu, Karate, Savate, Yawara, Aikido, Ate-Waza*. Thor Publishing Company, 1969.

———. *Complete Book of Judo*. Thor Publishing Company, 1973.

———. *Karate and Judo Exercises: Physical Conditioning for the Oriental Sport Fighting Arts*. Thor Publishing Company, 1972.

———. *Kung Fu and Tai Chi: Chinese Karate and Classical Exercise*. Thor Publishing Company, 1968.

Tohei, K. *Aikido in Daily Life*. Wehman Brothers, 1972.

———. *This Is Aikido*. Wehman Brothers, 1974.

———. *What Is Aikido?* Wehman Brothers, 1973.

Trias, Robert A. *The Hand Is My Sword: A Karate Handbook*. Charles E. Tuttle Company, 1973.

Watanabe, Jiichi, and Lindy Avakian. *The Secrets of Judo*. Charles E. Tuttle Company, 1959.

Watts, Alan. *The Way of Zen*. Random House, 1959.

APPENDIX C

DIRECTORY

Atlanta

Schools: Black Belt School of Judo, 3219 Cain Hill Place N.W.
              Highland Karate & Judo Club, 818 North Highland Avenue N.E.
              Joe Corley Karate Studios, 3160 Peachtree Road N.E.
Equipment: Atlanta Black Belt Academy, 4600-A Memorial Drive, Decatur.

Boston

Schools: Academy of Self-Defense, 240 Tremont Street.
              Boston Kempo Karate Club, 40 Boylston Street.
              Chinese Cultural Center, 651 Beacon Street.
              New England China Martial Arts Association, 15 Edinboro
                  Street *or* 117 Causeway Street.
Equipment: Suk Chang Institute of Tae Kwon Do, 1230 Massachusetts
                  Avenue, Cambridge.
              Zuber & Company, Inc., 1556 Commonwealth Avenue, Brigh-
                  ton.

Chicago

Schools: Chicago Judo & Karate Centers, 11307 South Michigan *or* 5814
                  Cermak Cicero.

Military Arts Institute, Inc., 3249 North Ashland.

Safe-Way Judo & Karate, 4715 South Ashland.

Equipment: East-West Market Exchange, 5449 North Broadway.

North Chicago Judo & Karate, 3508 South Holsted.

Van Boskirk, 7334 South Holsted.

Cleveland

Schools: Jim McLain's Karate & Self-Defense Studio, 689 Broadway.

Kim's Judo & Karate School, 21531 Lorain, Fairview Park.

Moon's Institute of Karate, 7527 Mentor *or* 9404 Madison.

Ohio Judo & Karate Association, 27820 Chagrin Boulevard *or* 11722 Detroit.

Equipment: Ohio Import Company, 2184 Noble.

Wolverine Brand Judo & Karate Uniform Supply, Inc., 3434 Memphis.

Clifton, New Jersey

School: Ed Kaloudis School of Koekian Karate, 1245 Main Avenue.

Dallas

Schools: Ahn's Karate School, 5221 West Lovers' Lane.

Dallas School of Karate, 2010 Commerce Street.

Gentle Earth Gung-Fu and Tai-Chi, 3409 Rosedale Street.

Tamura Judo Institute, 6907 Preston Road.

Equipment: Great American Imports, 4322 Buena Vista.

Ed Parker's Kempo Karate Studio, Amerada Plaza Shopping Center.

Detroit

Schools: Budokan Judo Club, 7811 Chase Dearborn.

Institute of Fighting Arts, Inc., 16213 West 7 Mile Road.

Kung-Fu/Karate Studios, 14013 West 8 Mile Road.

North American Aikido & Karate Club, 3345 West Davison Road.

Equipment: U.S. Karate Health Spas, Inc., 1134 South Woodward, Royal Oak.

Los Angeles

Schools: Academy of Martial Arts, 1128 South Western Avenue.
Aikido Institute of America, 3302 West Jefferson Boulevard.
Choi-Lai-Fut Kung-Fu Studio, 719 North Virgil Avenue.
International Karate Association, 4945 Hollywood Boulevard.

Equipment: Martial Arts Supplies Company, 10711 Venice Boulevard.
Nozawa Trading, Inc., 2534 West Pico Boulevard.

Miami

Schools: Dickinson School of Judo, 8858 S.W. 129th Street.
Samurai Judo-Karate School, 8464 S.W. 24th Street.
School of Kung-Fu, 2347 Coral Way.
Tracy's Karate & Judo Studios, 6469 S.W. 8th Street *or* 8247
    South Dixie Highway.

Equipment: Mertens' Martial Market, 1505 N.E. 26th Street, Fort Lauder-
    dale.

New York

Schools: Aikido of Uyeshiba, 142 West 18th Street.
Chaka Zulu's Nisei Goju Karate School, 93 Second Avenue.
Charles Nelson School of Self-Defense, 151 West 72nd Street.
John Kuhl's Combat Karate Academy, 231 East 86th Street.
New York Karate Academy, 1717 Broadway.
William C. C. Chen School of T'ai Chi Ch'uan, 161 West 23rd
    Street.

Equipment: Castello Combative Sports Company, 836 Broadway.
Honda Associates, Inc., 485 Fifth Avenue.

Philadelphia

Schools: American Karate Studios, Inc., 1552 Wadsworth Avenue.
Ishikawa Judo Club, 329 North Broad Street.
Martial Arts Studios, 2106 South Broad Street.
Philadelphia Aikikai, 1225 Arch Street.

Equipment: Lee Jong Sae, 6814 Old York Road.
Mahn Suh Park Tae Kyun Institute, 5749 North Broad Street.

San Francisco

Schools: Martial Arts, Inc., 5401 Mission Street.

      San Francisco Judo Institute, 2530 Taraval Street.

      San Francisco School of Karate, 1916 Polk Street *or* 1963 Ocean Avenue.

      Zen Budokai School of Self-Defense, 1819 Market Street.

Equipment: Central Sales Company, 4345 Cabrillo Street.

      Mutual Supply Company, 1090 Sansome Street.

Washington, D.C.

Schools: Bregman's Judo & Karate Center, 325 Pennsylvania Avenue S.E.

      Kung-Fu Karate Studio, 715 G Street N.W.

      Lin's Kung-Fu, 6119 Georgia Avenue N.W.

      YMCA Central Branch, 1736 G Street N.W.

SOLD